D1187941

SHAKESPEARE IN HINDSIGHT

EDINBURGH CRITICAL STUDIES IN SHAKESPEARE AND PHILOSOPHY

Series Editor: Kevin Curran

Edinburgh Critical Studies in Shakespeare and Philosophy takes seriously the speculative and world-making properties of Shakespeare's art. Maintaining a broad view of 'philosophy' that accommodates first-order questions of metaphysics, ethics, politics and aesthetics, the series also expands our understanding of philosophy to include the unique kinds of theoretical work carried out by performance and poetry itself. These scholarly monographs will reinvigorate Shakespeare studies by opening new interdisciplinary conversations among scholars, artists and students.

Published Titles

Rethinking Shakespeare's Political Philosophy: From Lear to Leviathan
Alex Schulman

Shakespeare in Hindsight: Counterfactual Thinking and Shakespearean Tragedy
Amir Khan

Forthcoming Titles

Shakespeare's Fugitive Politics
Thomas P. Anderson

Making Publics in Shakespeare's Playhouse
Paul Yachnin

Derrida Reads Shakespeare
Chiara Alfano

The Play and the Thing: A Phenomenology of Shakespearean Theatre
Matthew Wagner

SHAKESPEARE IN HINDSIGHT

Counterfactual Thinking and
Shakespearean Tragedy

◆ ◆ ◆

AMIR KHAN

EDINBURGH
University Press

© Amir Khan, 2016

Edinburgh University Press Ltd
The Tun – Holyrood Road,
12(2f) Jackson's Entry,
Edinburgh EH8 8PJ
www.euppublishing.com

Typeset in 11/13 Adobe Sabon by
IDSUK (DataConnection) Ltd, and
printed and bound in Great Britain by
CPI Group (UK) Ltd, Croydon CR0 4YY

A CIP record for this book is available from the British Library

ISBN 978 1 4744 0945 2 (hardback)
ISBN 978 1 4744 0946 9 (webready PDF)
ISBN 978 1 4744 0947 6 (epub)

CONTENTS

ACKNOWLEDGEMENTS

This book would have been impossible without the Social Sciences and Humanities Research Council of Canada Doctoral Fellowship and the Ontario Graduate Scholarship. Prior to these, I was fortunate enough to make my way through the now defunct summer-student programme at Alcan Aluminium Smelters Ltd. (and endorsed by then Canadian Auto Workers Local 2301). It was no choice of mine to grow up in Kitimat, British Columbia, but I managed to finance my early years of graduate study by virtue of this single, strange contingency (and by virtue also of repairing studs in the rebuild shop).

Teachers and professors are supposed to inspire, and many pushed me forward and along. Teachers I would like to thank are Dave Durrant and Grant Frater. Professors I would like to mention are Eric Levy, Dennis Danielson, Ashok Aklujkar, Steven Savitt, Alex Dick, Richard van Oort and Michael Zeitlin, all of whom I knew at the University of British Columbia; Stephen Pender, Tom Dilworth and Richard Douglass-Chin at the University of Windsor; at the University of Ottawa, Janice Fiamengo, David Staines, Irena Makaryk, Victoria Burke, Bernhard Radloff and David Sacks. Ian Dennis, my dissertation supervisor, was a superb ally during my time in Ottawa. Contingencies have changed the name on the dedication page, but in some counterfactual world it remains his.

Other professional colleagues I'd like to thank, and whom I've seen several times on the conference circuit, are Eric Gans, Andrew Bartlett, Adam Katz, Chris Fleming, John O'Carroll, Matthew Schneider, Matthew Taylor, Peter Goldman and Sandor Goodhart. Also, Larry Jackson and Adam Gonya, as well as Sérgio Dias Branco, all of whom I know more 'virtually', if less personally. I would especially like to thank Michael Fischer for making the long trip up north to my defence. And those editors who have taken a chance on my work – perfectly willing, I mean, to accommodate some of my unusual digressions – have all helped me to achieve, by allowing me to put down in print, some version of my best self. These editors are (once again) Eric Gans, Susan Fast, Stan Hawkins, Gary Morris, Scott Forsyth, Susan Morrison, Gail Kern Paster and Kevin Curran.

I've had to lean on my mother more than I would have liked since leaving Ottawa, but her love and sacrifice go well beyond my time out of school. Her devotion to her children and grandchildren is peerless. To my kind-hearted and generous siblings, Raheel and Sarah: I am fortunate to be cut from the same cloth as you without rivalry. Others more family than friends are Noah Richmond, Jonas Ng, Zachariah Schnier, Nitin Kumar and A.S. Dhillon. I love you all.

Lastly to my daughter Arden, to whom this book is dedicated. A tempest struck while I was writing this. I am sorry for it. I can only hope the words which appear here will one day reduce some of the painful distance between us. I love you very much.

A NOTE ON TEXTS

All references to Shakespeare's plays are to *The Norton Shakespeare*, eds Stephen Greenblatt et al. (New York: W.W. Norton, 1997).

SERIES EDITOR'S PREFACE

Picture Macbeth alone on stage, staring intently into empty space. 'Is this a dagger which I see before me?' he asks, grasping decisively at the air. On one hand, this is a quintessentially theatrical question. At once an object and a vector, the dagger describes the possibility of knowledge ('Is this a dagger') in specifically visual and spatial terms ('which I see before me?'). At the same time, Macbeth is posing a quintessentially *philosophical* question, one that assumes knowledge to be both conditional and experiential, and that probes the relationship between certainty and perception as well as intention and action. It is from this shared ground of art and inquiry, of theatre and theory, that this series advances its basic premise: *Shakespeare is philosophical.*

It seems like a simple enough claim. But what does it mean exactly, beyond the parameters of this specific moment in *Macbeth*? Does it mean that Shakespeare had something we could think of as his own philosophy? Does it mean that he was influenced by particular philosophical schools, texts, and thinkers? Does it mean, conversely, that modern philosophers have been influenced by *him*, that Shakespeare's plays and poems have been, and continue to be, resources for philosophical thought and speculation?

The answer is 'yes' all around. These are all useful ways of conceiving a philosophical Shakespeare and all point to lines of inquiry that this series welcomes. But Shakespeare is philosophical in a much more fundamental way as well. Shakespeare is philosophical because the plays and poems actively create new worlds of knowledge and new scenes of ethical encounter. They ask big questions, make bold arguments, and develop new vocabularies in order to think what might otherwise be unthinkable. Through both their scenarios and their imagery, the plays and poems engage the qualities of consciousness, the consequences of human action, the phenomenology of motive and attention, the conditions of personhood, and the relationship among different orders of reality and experience. This is writing and dramaturgy, moreover, that consistently experiments with a broad range of conceptual crossings, between love and subjectivity, nature and politics, and temporality and form.

Edinburgh Critical Studies in Shakespeare and Philosophy takes seriously these speculative and world-making dimensions of Shakespeare's work. The series proceeds from a core conviction that art's capacity to think – to formulate, not just reflect, ideas – is what makes it urgent and valuable. Art matters because, unlike other human activities, it establishes its own frame of reference, reminding us that all acts of creation – biological, political, intellectual, and amorous – are grounded in imagination. This is a far cry from business-as-usual in Shakespeare studies. Because historicism remains the methodological gold standard of the field, far more energy has been invested in exploring what Shakespeare once meant than in thinking rigorously about what Shakespeare continues to make possible. In response, Edinburgh Critical Studies in Shakespeare and Philosophy pushes back against the critical orthodoxies of historicism and cultural studies to clear a space for scholarship that confronts aspects of literature that can neither be reduced to, nor adequately explained by, particular historical contexts.

Shakespeare's creations are not just inheritances of a past culture, frozen artefacts whose original settings must be expertly reconstructed in order to be understood. The plays and poems are also living art, vital thought-worlds that struggle, across time, with foundational questions of metaphysics, ethics, politics, and aesthetics. With this orientation in mind, Edinburgh Critical Studies in Shakespeare and Philosophy offers a series of scholarly monographs that will reinvigorate Shakespeare studies by opening new interdisciplinary conversations among scholars, artists, and students.

Kevin Curran

To Arden, my perdita

CHAPTER 1

INTRODUCTION

Negative capability, that is when man is capable of being in uncertainties, mysteries, doubts, without any irritable reaching after fact and reason – Coleridge, for instance, would let go by a fine isolated verisimilitude caught from the Penetralium of mystery, from being incapable of remaining content with half knowledge.

John Keats

Now to me the total works of Shakespeare are like a very, very complete set of codes and these codes, cipher for cipher, set off in us, stir in us, vibrations and impulses which we immediately try to make coherent and understandable.

Peter Brook

Discussing tragedy is tricky business. One is immediately tempted to outline a definition of tragedy, or, at the very least, to account for certain criteria that allow it to function. What this project proposes instead are reading strategies that will allow a 'tragic effect' to resonate. In particular, this project makes a case for reading 'in the present', what Stanley Cavell calls inhabiting 'an experience of *continuous presentness*'.[1] The most expedient way to do this will be to consider alternative possibilities to the accepted linear (narrative) developments of the plays at hand: assuming Macbeth had done *x* instead of *y*, for example, or that we, as readers, know *x* and not *y*. Yet this not in order to get away from the narrative unfolding of a play but, on the contrary, to become more intimate with it. These readings will be defined, somewhat loosely, as 'counterfactual' readings. Furthermore, the tragic effect will be linked to 'discovery'– what Northrop Frye, and before him Aristotle, calls '*anagnorisis*' – emphasising in particular a sense of 'wonder'. This project argues that (1) the sorts of discoveries to be made are those that reveal or sustain a sense of wonder, the 'uncertainties, mysteries, doubts' that Keats associates with 'negative capability', and (2) this sense of wonder is key to the functioning of tragedy. Therefore, what is to be discovered cannot be prescribed because if we articulate beforehand just what it is we are looking for, we have removed ourselves from the realm of negative capability and, just because of that, the tragic effect is lost. One could make the case that these plays, in order to be tragic, must *initiate* a discovery procedure. This could be a criterion. Yet what we find in no way accounts for tragedy but merely reminds us of the possibilities open to a tragic play.

A.C. Bradley's *Shakespearean Tragedy* isolates a particular literary device (*hamartia*, also taken from Aristotle) and links it to the functioning of tragedy. In Bradley's estimation, tragedy is inescapably tied to character. We can no longer conceive of tragedy without first discovering a tragic character, and then discovering that character's 'tragic trait'.[2] Yet the trait or flaw in question does not originate at any specific point in the narrative but governs the unfolding of the entire play. Othello is not thought to *become* jealous because he is egged on by Iago. His tragic flaw is that he *is* jealous. Just because of this, we are never allowed to ask – hence to discover, for ourselves – when exactly *we* are convinced of Othello's jealousy. Bradley's criticism makes such a question specious. What do we lose when we know that Othello is jealous? We lose, first and foremost, our presentness to the play. 'Presentness' is here defined as an immediate intimacy to the particular unfolding of the play, where we as readers are uncertain of what comes next. If, as will be argued here, the articulation of tragedy is linked to an articulation of the conditions of our present experience of a play, then what an application of Bradley's criticism has managed, in fact, is to negate a discussion of tragedy.

Moreover, 'presentness' as here conceived does not denote the isolation and analysis of present social conditions which mediate our relationship to the play from without.[3] Rather, 'presentness' emphasises an experience of the play that coalesces around contingencies internal to the play itself. A 'present' reading is present to the immediate narrative unfolding of the play and questions whether one set of events or conditions is destined to occur instead of another. The 'presentness' to be established is, first and foremost, the reader's, but then only through the convincing subjective claiming of possibilities suggested either by a specific character or by what is taken to be the specific conventions internal to the world of the play. The types of knowledge afforded us as readers within the play, e.g. about the past (the Ghost in *Hamlet*), or about the future (the prophecy in *Macbeth*), bear on how we consider the possible (as we shall see). This is not to say that a consideration of external tragic convention in limiting what Shakespeare could or could not have done is not worth attending to. But asking ourselves how and why Shakespeare may have chosen to end a play one way and not another is not the end of the discussion, merely the beginning. To assume that Shakespeare was limited by formal constraints of genre is not necessarily hasty but does more to quash a discussion of possibilities than foster it.

The linking of presentness to tragedy is intuited by George Steiner in his claim that the 'metaphysics of Christianity and

Marxism'[4] make the rendering of tragedy impossible because the narrative contiguity of these 'configurations of belief'[5] presupposes redemption. This belief in redemption is not necessarily utopian. Rather, the means to its achievement depend on reason or understanding. We are to believe (through an understanding of God's divine plan or the rational unfolding of the dialectic) what Cavell says in his discussion of *King Lear* – namely, that we can 'save our lives by knowing them'.[6] In seeking to know, in this case, not our lives but those of the characters before us – and then by appealing to external dialectics – we are removing ourselves from their presentness and subsequently the presentness of the play at hand.

Any a priori knowledge applied to the play after the fact risks such removal. Because Bradley's formulation or discovery of a character's tragic flaw occurs beyond the text, it can only be applied a priori and in hindsight. It may be compelling enough to discover that all plays we consider tragic seem to have a character who possesses a tragic flaw. However, this does not explain why we felt the play tragic in the first place lacking this prior knowledge. This may indeed be because the more we think about tragic plays the more likely we are to move from the 'unknown to the known',[7] reflecting Aristotle's original definition of *anagnorisis*; though where he was talking about the discovery made by a particular character in a play (say, Oedipus's discovery of his fate, linked closely to *peripeteia*), what this project seeks to emphasise is a move from unknown to known occurring at certain removes from the text. This version of *anagnorisis* has more in common with Frye's reformulation of the term.

> When a reader of a novel asks 'How is this story going to turn out?' he is asking a question about the plot, specifically about that crucial aspect of the plot Aristotle calls discovery or *anagnorisis*. But he is equally likely to ask, 'What's the point of this story?'[8]

Though Frye himself does not digress on the gravity of his reformulation, Terence Cave elaborates on Frye's achievement:

> [Frye's] definition assigns *anagnorisis* to 'us', they readers or spectators: we recognize the unifying shape of the whole design ... In one sense, what he is doing here is parallel to the accounts of *peripeteia* in which the 'surprise' it occasions is the spectators' rather than the characters': *anagnorisis* is the structural feature producing an effect outside the fiction. But the effect in this instance isn't purely local. It shifts the whole reading from a linear, narrative movement to a grasping of 'unifying shape' and 'simultaneous significance'; plot gives way to theme and interpretation. This appropriation by the reader of *anagnorisis* as a recognition both of overall form and of thematic coherence is a radical manoeuvre.[9]

The penetralium of experience is now open to discussion of theme and interpretation rather than consideration of the linear movement of narrative. But Frye's reformulation of *anagnorisis* does not immediately place us in a play's continuous present. Even if a character's internal discovery procedure is superseded by the reader discovery, the consideration of theme also occurs in hindsight and begs the reader to seek something out after the fact. For example, G.W. Knight's influential interpretation locates the meaning of *Hamlet* in 'death',[10] or, more precisely, nominates death as the 'predominating human theme ... suffused through the whole play'.[11] Though he is less explicit about what makes the play tragic, it would not be unfair to assume that Knight thought tragedy more accessible to thematic interpretation (and less to specific character criticism). Yet in seeking to explain the play in this way, he errs precisely as Bradley does. He provides a reading of the play that can only be applied post facto, thereby removing us from the presentness of the play and its tragedy. By explaining the 'atmosphere'[12] that governs the play, Knight, like Bradley, has explained tragedy away.

The obvious objection at this point is that *all* criticism is done in such a 'post-facto' manner. Certainly we must read the plays in their entirety before commenting on specific occurrences. Even Aristotle, when considering discoveries made by a character at certain points in the narrative, did so not outside of, or beyond, knowledge of the play as a whole. Aristotle's version of *anagnorisis* provides an immediate narrative intimacy to the play lacking in Frye's. Yet Frye's provides an understanding that the reader must claim, or appropriate, a discovery about a play as his or her own – though not by articulating the thematic criteria which allow a tragedy to function, but by being open to other (narrative) possibilities the play, at once, hints at and (through the progression of the narrative) *denies*. This project argues that these possibilities are best housed in what Frye calls an 'anagogic'[13] universe of both poetry *and* criticism. The discovery of textual possibilities and reader assumptions *lost* is how the term *anagnorisis* is to be used here. Because there can be no limit to the sorts of suggestions a play makes at any given point in its narrative, the subjective and convincing claiming of these hypothetical alternatives could also be counted as a criterion for the effective articulation of tragedy, which is to say an effective articulation of one's presentness to a play. This particular criterion of *anagnorisis* does not prescribe what a reader ought to look for but merely models a strategy of reading – say, a strategy of scepticism towards our inherited assumptions about a given play. Finally, this project does not take issue with post-facto criticism per se. What it attempts to show is how such readings, imposed on texts after the fact, are deleterious to a reader reception of tragedy.

For example, Stephen Greenblatt's historicist approach to the plays can highlight the sense of wonder Shakespeare himself may have intended to elicit from his audiences. Commenting on *King Lear*, Greenblatt's assessment of the historical contingencies surrounding the narrative assumptions of Elizabethan audiences is pertinent:

> Why does [Shakespeare's] Lear, who has, as the play begins, already drawn up the map equitably dividing the kingdom, stage the love test? In Shakespeare's principal source, an anonymous play called *The True Chronicle History of King Leir* ... there is a gratifyingly clear answer. Leir's strong-willed daughter Cordelia has vowed that she will marry only a man whom she herself loves; Leir wishes her to marry the man he chooses for his own dynastic purposes. He stages the love test, anticipating that in competing with her sisters, Cordelia will declare that she loves her father best, at which point Leir will demand that she prove her love by marrying the suitor of his choice. The stratagem backfires, but its purpose is clear. By stripping his character of a comparable motive, Shakespeare makes Lear's act seem stranger, at once more arbitrary and more rooted in deep psychological needs.[14]

We see that Shakespeare sought to undermine and play with audience expectations, indeed to make Lear 'seem stranger' and 'more arbitrary'. Yet this bit of knowledge does not ally us with Elizabethan audiences because the narrative contingencies surrounding *The True Chronicle History of King Leir* are no longer resonant in our present-day experience of the text. If reading Shakespeare's play today elicits a comparable sense of awe and wonder, it is precisely *not* because of any prior knowledge of what Lear (Leir) is expected to do. Indeed, there is simply no guarantee, today, that Lear's initial motives *will* seem arbitrary and strange in staging the love test as he does. Elizabethan audiences may have had reason to doubt Lear's motives in

Act 1, scene 1. A reader nowadays has little reason to do so unless he or she brings knowledge of Lear's madness to the play before reading it. What readers nowadays must do is decide, for themselves, if and when exactly Lear's madness takes hold.

Greenblatt's historical explanation applies to Elizabethan audiences only. It does not follow that we feel a comparable sense of awe and mystery at Lear's motives at the same point in the narrative. As an explanation for a present-day reception of the text, this knowledge is clearly inadequate. Moreover, such historicising risks lulling us into the belief that because Elizabethan audiences were sceptical of Lear's motives at this particular point in the narrative, *we too are justified in assuming Lear to be mad in Act 1, scene 1*. Greenblatt's reflections ought to initiate a second look at our own assumptions about the play, hence an attempt to locate where exactly we are likely to believe Lear mad. What happens instead is we feel validated by this bit of historical exegesis. We feel the same sense of awe and mystery at the unfolding of events. But Greenblatt's explanation becomes a cause rather than an effect, as though our present-day understanding of the text somehow inherits this bit of historical knowledge.

In the opening pages of his *Shakespearean Negotiations*, Greenblatt says that the most 'satisfying intensity'[15] he feels as a reader of literature comes from reading Shakespeare. Greenblatt is seeking to account not for an intensity associated with Shakespearean tragedy, but for an intensity he associates with a confrontation between the text in hand and the 'totalizing society'[16] in which the text was bred. The particular makeup of such a society encompasses, most immediately, 'religious and state bureaucracy',[17] so that an understanding of the interplay between a work of art and its existence within the fabric of religious and state institutions is a necessary condition to account for its power, or 'social energy'.[18] Such confrontations, though historically specific, 'continu[e] to generate the illusion of life for centuries'.[19]

One immediate objection to this strategy arises from knowing, or feeling, that we are just as likely to react to the power of Shakespeare's play *before* making the sort of historical discoveries that Greenblatt would have us commit to. Greenblatt himself is sensitive to this:

> Does this mean that the aesthetic power of a play like *King Lear* is a direct transmission from Shakespeare's time to our own? Certainly not. That play and the circumstances in which it was originally embedded have been continuously, often radically, refigured. But these refigurations do not cancel history, locking us into a perpetual present; on the contrary, they are signs of the inescapability of a historical process, a structured negotiation and exchange, already evident in the initial moments of empowerment. That there is no direct, unmediated link between ourselves and Shakespeare's plays does not mean that there is no link at all. The 'life' that literary works seem to possess long after both the death of the author and the death of the culture for which the author wrote is the historical consequence, however transformed and refashioned, of the social energy initially encoded in those works.[20]

Articulating the historical realities surrounding a play is one way to account for its social energy. Indeed, such discoveries can be both illuminating and liberating. But do we really believe that the power of Shakespeare's plays, upon reading them *for the first time*, resides in some secret, even 'coded' negotiations going on that we are not exactly privy to in the present, but which reside in our present experience of the play nonetheless? Such reasoning is dubious and confuses cause and effect. That is, this sort of historical commentary is an *effect* of the power of Shakespeare's plays and not the cause, as Greenblatt would have us believe.

'Presentness' obviously denotes the temporal, our aware-ness or experience of time or time passing. But the time is the sort internal to the play – not the sort where we know, from without, that one thing is going to happen rather than another. It is the time, or perception of time, linked to being in ignorance of the world, to discovering, rather than chart-ing out, its rhythms. Only when we don't know what is going to happen are we attuned to the present. So the temporal ele-ment denoted here by presentness also denotes a narrative or affective intimacy predicated not on seeing the narrative play out as we expect (as in, arguably, melodrama), but on expe-riencing it as yet to be written. Furthermore, as mentioned previously, the nature of reader presentness to a play is fun-damentally altered from within the play itself – for example, based on prior knowledge from the world of the play (the testimony of a ghost, as in *Hamlet*), or on knowledge about the future (a prophecy, as in *Macbeth*). Far from being need-lessly cryptic here, to propose the achievement of presentness as a legitimate goal for literary criticism is to propose a task 'as rigorous as ... any spiritual exercise'.[21] Some measure of historical forgetting is in order. Rather than assume that such forgetting is all too common, this project assumes that such forgetting is exceptionally difficult. How can we possibly read Shakespeare, nowadays, for the first time?

An answer has been hinted at thus far, which is to accept what Greenblatt summarily dismisses. If we accept, that is, that our experience of a play *does* come from being locked into a 'perpetual present', we begin to understand that an articulation of the conditions of presentness is necessary to account for the power of Shakespeare's tragedies. But how to account for the presentness of a text and avoid the pitfalls of post-facto criticising or historicising?

The use of 'counterfactual' discussion in history, for example, has been taken up by Niall Ferguson. In his *Virtual History*, he gathers together nine historians and has each explore counterfactual alternatives to a major historical event. The essays are drawn-out thought experiments, and, though informed by rigorous research, are (obviously) highly speculative. The point is not to arrive at a definitive counterfactual reading, but to understand better the ramifications of such thinking in *this* world. Geoffrey Hawthorn (1991) highlights a minimal ethic guiding the enterprise of counterfactual reasoning. He notes that '[e]xplanations ... are not fixed' and that to 'consider the possibilities suggested in explanation ... [is] thereby [to] enhance our understanding'.[22] Furthermore, the 'narrative fallacy'[23] expounded on at length by Nassim Nicholas Taleb in *The Black Swan* suggests that isolating cause-and-effect relationships, whether personal or historical, leads us to make speculative judgements about the future anyway. Taleb calls this 'our vulnerability to overinterpretation and ... predilection for compact stories over raw truths'.[24] One starting assumption this project makes is that the narrative fallacy is not to be avoided, but *multiplied*. Here is Daniel Kahneman on Taleb:

In *The Black Swan*, Taleb introduced the notion of a narrative fallacy to describe how flawed stories of the past shape our views of the world and our expectations for the future. Narrative fallacies arrive inevitably from our continuous attempt to make sense of the world. The explanatory stories that people find compelling are simple; are concrete rather than abstract; assign a larger role to talent, stupidity, and intentions than to luck; and focus on a few striking events that happened rather than on the countless events that failed to happen. Any recent salient event is a candidate to become the kernel of a causal narrative. Taleb suggests that we humans constantly fool ourselves by constructing

flimsy accounts of the past and believing they are true ...
A compelling narrative fosters an illusion of inevitability.
Consider the story of ... Google. Two creative graduate
students in the computer science department at Stanford
university come up with a superior way of searching information on the Internet. They seek and obtain funding to
start a company and make a series of decisions that work
out well. Within a few years, the company they started is
one of the most valuable stocks in America, and the two
former graduate students are among the richest people on
the planet....

   I intentionally told this story blandly, but you get the
idea: there is a very good story here. Fleshed out in more
detail, the story could give you the sense that you understand what made Google succeed; it would also make you
feel that you have learned a valuable general lesson about
what makes businesses succeed. Unfortunately, there is
good reason to believe that your sense of understanding
and learning ... is largely illusory. The ultimate test of an
explanation is whether it would have made the event predictable in advance. No story of Google's unlikely success
will meet that test, because no story can include the myriad
of events that would have caused a different outcome. The
human mind does not deal well with nonevents. The fact
that many of the important events that did occur involve
choices further tempts you to exaggerate the role of skill
and underestimate the part that luck played in the outcome. Because every critical decision turned out well, the
record suggests almost flawless prescience – but bad luck
could have disrupted any one of the successful steps.[25]

Annexing this critique of narrative to our understanding
of tragedy, one could say 'because every decision turned
out so poorly, the record suggests tragedy – but good
luck could have disrupted any one of the disastrous steps'.
The goal here is not necessarily to 'flesh out' complete

counterfactual worlds, but to begin, at the very least, to consider alternatives.

Furthermore, what Taleb and Kahneman call the 'narrative fallacy' calls into question the authority of *any* established narrative, or, at the very least, makes 'the' narrative as contingent on a certain outcome of events as any other. Taken to the extreme, favouring any one narrative over another leads to a sort of fatalism, or belief in historical necessity. The idea behind using counterfactual alternatives is to force the mind to consider *non-events*, which is to remind the reader (of Shakespearean tragedy) that the characters on the page are free individuals.

For example, note Hegel's remarks on *Hamlet*:

[W]e may see the tragic issue also merely in the light of the effect of unhappy circumstances and external accidents, which might have brought about, quite as readily, a different result and a happy conclusion. ... Such a course of events can insistently arrest our attention; but in the result it can only be horrible, and the demand is direct and irresistible that the external accidents ought to accord with that which is identical with the spiritual nature of such noble characters. Only as thus regarded can we feel ourselves reconciled with the grievous end of *Hamlet* .... From a purely external point of view, the death of Hamlet appears as an accident occasioned by his duel with Laertes and the interchange of the daggers. But in the background of Hamlet's soul, death is already present from the first. The sandbank of finite condition will not content his spirit. As the focus of such mourning and weakness, such melancholy, such a loathing of all the conditions of life, we feel from the first that, hemmed within such an environment of horror, he is a lost man, whom the surfeit of the soul has well-nigh already done to death before death itself approaches him from without.[26]

This is a clear example of the sort of fatalism mentioned earlier. Because we know Hamlet is destined to perish at the hands of contingency, it is for reasons of consolation and comfort that we assume he is doomed from the outset.

To this sort of post-facto criticism, Hegel ties the 'tragic conclusion'. Yet once again, as an explanation of tragedy, such criticism merely explains tragedy away and denies the tragic effect's relationship to presentness. Nor does explaining what might have happened had Hamlet avoided Laertes's swipe necessarily make the tragic effect more resonant. Considering its possibility merely reminds us that no law dictates that Hamlet was destined to perish. Oscillating between a consideration of what actually happens and what could have happened is to inhabit the realm of tragedy and elicits in the imagination a sense of mystery, awe and wonder. The so-called 'comfort' we feel when reading tragedy occurs not because tragedy makes sense, has a moral, but because it reminds us that there is no moral, that human lives and fates are subject to contingencies beyond our control.

This sort of thinking is anathema to that championed by Hegel, the 'dialectical' unfolding that has had scholars since 1807 trying to articulate a definitive version of *the* narrative that dictates the course of our lives (whether based on class, religion, nationality, or, more recently, culture, gender and race). It is beyond the scope of this study to delineate the sorts of assumptions and biases created by the narrative tendency in general. This project is not historiography. What this project focuses on is the effect of post-facto narration and historicising on reading Shakespearean tragedy.

Cavell's idea of continuous presentness is rooted in the reading, and less in the viewing, of Shakespeare's plays. Though elsewhere he hints that tragedy is enhanced in viewing a character on stage (thereby participating, directly, in that character's presence), the achievement of putting poetry to narrative – perfected, he says, by Shakespeare[27] –

ultimately gives us the feeling of a world unfolding before us rather than merely behaving according to convention. Comparing the achievement of Shakespeare's poetry to music, Cavell says

> [i]t is not uncommon to find Shakespeare's plays compared to music, but in the instances I have seen, this comparison rests upon more or less superficial features of music, for example, on its balance of themes, it recurrences, shifts of mood, climaxes – in a word, on its theatrical properties. But music is ... dramatic in a more fundamental sense, or it became so when it no longer expanded festivals or enabled dancing or accompanied songs, but achieved its own dramatic autonomy, worked out its progress in its own terms.[28]

The 'dramatic autonomy' Cavell describes in music is the move to tonality and the sonata form.[29] Shakespeare achieves an analogous dramatic autonomy in putting verse to narrative, which means, in a sense, that the working out of contingencies occurs within the play itself, is less subordinate to outside influences (its 'theatrical properties', or, in the case of music, as an appendage to 'festivals' or 'dancing'). This may be reason enough to make the case *for* a type of narrative necessity, as if, in the very achievement of this sort of autonomy, the case for whatever does happen is guaranteed by the internal power and 'directedness'[30] of the play's particular language. But what such poetry manages to achieve is an 'imitat[ion] [of] the simplest facts of life',[31] an understanding that 'life is lived in time', which means 'that what will happen is not here and now and yet may be settled by what is happening here and now in a way we cannot know or will not see here and now'.[32] By calling for a break from convention in favour of a dramatic autonomy that places us in the here and how, Cavell is encouraging us 'to let the past go and to let the future take its time'.[33]

The question of page versus stage, or reading versus viewing, will be dealt with more intimately in Chapter 3. For now, suffice it to say that Shakespeare's words, passing either before our eyes on the page, or past our ears on the stage, tune us into the present. So the unfolding of a particular type of speech, either written or spoken, which captures certain rhythms of a life lived in time is another criterion of presentness and hence of tragedy. Yet once we are awake to the present, another criterion of tragedy, as a logical extension of poetry's ability to mark time in narrative form, is the nature of the words themselves – that is, their *suggestiveness*. Marjorie Garber is not the first to comment on the inexhaustibility of Shakespeare's texts:

> The plays are tough, durable, rich, flexible, capacious, and endlessly evocative. They are also provocative, alluring, suggestive, and challenging.... That these plays can sustain so many powerful and persuasive interpretations is in fact as close as I can come to explaining the elusive nature of their greatness.[34]

Shakespeare's achievement, aided not only by the anomaly of our knowing nothing about the man's personal views, but also by the sheer range of his output, is that he created a universe in which anything can be said to exist and nothing. This again suggests that Shakespeare's plays, and more importantly his language, are in a privileged position to sustain a discussion of possibilities. The suggestiveness of the language uttered by his characters gives voice not to the necessity of events as dictated by convention or narrative, but to the possibility of other outcomes.

David Scott Kastan notes that '[p]ain and loss remain the central tragic facts'[35] of Shakespeare's tragedies. One reason Shakespeare's tragic texts are particularly effective is not simply because of the sudden and seemingly gratuitous loss of life, but because of the gratuitous loss of possibilities – say, of human subjectivities. Shakespeare reminds us, more than other tragic poets, of the possibilities inherent in the characters he has created through their suggestive speech. Considering possibilities latent in speech is one way to immerse ourselves further in the Shakespearean universe.

For example, very early on in the play, just after discovering that he has been named Thane of Cawdor, Macbeth remarks: 'If chance will have me king, why, chance may crown me / Without my stir' (1.3.142–3).[36] The eerie possibility suggested in these lines is that it has *crossed Macbeth's mind* that he should *not* act. In our knowledge of how badly things are to turn out, we may be pleading for Macbeth simply to follow his own advice. The counterfactual question worth posing here is: what if Macbeth had chosen not to act? What manner of play would we have then? Would we still have a play? If the immediate answer is, 'Of course not!', the next step would be to ask why he does act, how and if the call to act, for Macbeth, restricts his agency or promotes it. Attending to such matters bears fruit, is a way of reading, rather than explaining, the play and its horrors. I present such a reading of *Macbeth* in Chapter 4.

Finally, one could argue that reading counterfactual alternatives into these plays actually moves us away from the plays. If, ultimately, the words on the page dramatically unfolding in time are what open up the penetralium of experience, then by focusing not on what is there, but on what isn't, we are moving away from presentness and hence from tragedy. But by being attuned to speech unfolding over time in such a way that we do not know what will happen next, what is being created in the mind is the space for a type of affective intimacy that exists only in the moment. The post-facto attempt to articulate this intimacy, by default, is drawn to what actually happens in the play via consideration of content. Yet the content to draw out is that *which does not exist* – that which, though suggested by speech, is, usually and from a position of hindsight, silenced. If it is merely the suggestiveness of speech articulated poetically in time that elicits presentness to events as they unfold, however, then shouldn't we be 'present' to all of Shakespeare's plays, not merely his tragedies?

The idea is that 'presentness' could only be enhanced by an ending we could not possibly want. Tragedies, more than comedies, elicit feelings of awe and wonder because when they end, we are left reeling unequivocally in the subjunctive mood. 'What if' questions are not posed with the same urgency with comedies (though, indeed, they *could* be posed). The true horror of tragedy entails an immediate desire to fight off a sense of affective vulnerability – to remove ourselves from the burden of its inexplicability, usually through explanation. The burden is of being entirely *too* present to these characters. For criticism of tragedy to remain homologous to that which it seeks to describe (rather than explain, or explain away), remaining in the subjunctive register is of paramount importance. Reader presentness is to be enhanced not only by considering the narrative or poetic power of Shakespeare's words, but also by considering the power of these plays to elicit thoughts about what didn't happen. Establishing reader presentness is a means of engaging with the burden of the (characters') present.

Susan Sontag calls tragedy an 'ennobling vision of nihilism',[37] a seemingly contradictory definition, for what could possibly be ennobling about meaninglessness? The equation of tragedy with nihilism, with a sort of aesthetic stasis, means that to discuss tragedy is to invite an end to discussion. Here, the tragic effect has something to do with what Stephen Booth calls a critical 'helplessness'.[38] Shakespeare critics, naturally, have to decide what to do with, or about, this feeling of helplessness. A common response is to try to locate the feeling, whether in the audience or in the play. To locate tragedy is not to make the tragic resonant in the reader imagination, however, but to circumvent feelings of helplessness – and then, for the sake of what?

For the sake of a discussion – to extend the life of a conversation about tragedy. To claim that the critical push towards historicism, particularly in Shakespeare studies, is directly related to feelings of critical helplessness is somewhat hasty. What historicism does, however, is locate our understanding of aesthetic pleasure in neither the play in hand nor in reader (or viewer) response, but in something *else* – namely, the social and cultural forces said to mediate the type of response already identified. In such a case, reader or viewer response is subordinate to consideration of such mediating forces. Such an approach is perhaps suitable to cultural historians but is rather inadequate to critics who want to have a discussion about tragedy *now*, the tragic effect itself, and not how it comes to be. Putting forward a project or critical strategy to make the tragic effect resonant in reader imagination means that setting aside those that locate the tragic effect in (foregone) historical realities is merely step one.

Nietzsche is not often thought of as a historian, but his critique of tragedy, locating it within an ancient schema of gods and Titans, seems to be a critique or disavowal of a critical component of tragedy – its intimate relationship to presentness. Yet Nietzsche's idea is that 'presentness' cannot occur in our present. Because we are at removes from certain historical contingencies that allow presentness to happen, we cannot hope to recover it, and this just because of our present (our present circumstances, whether social, economic or political). His idea of the 'birth' of tragedy overlaps with, and is not in opposition to, Steiner's later thesis of the 'death' of tragedy. Nietzsche says that tragedy is born not within a society that seeks to overcome the Dionysian (by branding it, as Christianity does, as 'evil'), but in a society, supremely optimistic, that embraces and celebrates what is otherwise thought to be its (own) destructive properties. Only in such a society can tragedy be 'ennobling'. Steiner, analogously, says tragedy is dead because we have moved away from 'myth'. Though 'the myths which have prevailed since Descartes and Newton are myths of reason',[39] such mythology is detrimental to art, let alone tragedy. The myth of reason encompasses the critical desire not to explain, but explain away. Tragedy, as an institution, is more readily located in the particular social makeup of ancient societies in which a belief in gods and giants is taken for granted because, in such a society, no ennobling or teleological vision of the human race *based on redemption* exists. With the death of pagan gods, so it follows, comes the death of tragedy and a type of corrupted optimism that seeks to repress the Dionysian element of tragedy. (This inverted view of optimism, in repressing rather than embracing Dionysus, is, for Nietzsche, a veritable transvaluation of values.) To avoid tragedy, our post-sacral, godless and secular order becomes one of shifting relativisms, each one likely to be verified and then abandoned in time, none carrying any concrete meaning, all encompassed by that dispiriting term, 'postmodernism'. What about such an order could possibly elicit the tragic? Undoubtedly, we have a vision of 'nihilism', and if we have *that*, part of the critical task to follow in wanting to make such a vision 'ennobling' is to make the tragic effect resonant in, hence necessarily tied to, present conditions of secular postmodernity.

Terry Eagleton's critique of Steiner is pertinent:

[T]ragedy, that privileged preserve of gods and spiritual giants, has now been decisively democratized – which is to say, for the devotees of gods and giants, abolished. Hence the death-of-tragedy thesis. Tragedy, however, did not vanish because there were no more great men. It did not expire with the last absolutist monarch. On the contrary, since under democracy each one of us is to be incommensurably cherished, it has been multiplied far beyond antique imagining ... Far from there being 'nothing democratic in the vision of tragedy', as George Steiner asserts, absolutely nobody is safe from tragedy in such a world. The Enlightenment, commonly thought to be the enemy of tragedy, is in fact a breeder of it. It is worth recalling that tragic art began in a society which called itself a democracy.[40]

If tragedy nowadays has indeed been multiplied far beyond antique imagining, the case is not that tragedy has simply disappeared but that greater (critical) efforts must be made to make it resonant. To say each life is, or has the potential to be, tragic means that expressing the truth of tragedy no longer occurs via the definitive account of its function across a particular cultural or interpretive community, but in the unique individual response to tragedy. How then to increase subjective claims to tragedy while still wanting to say, in the last instance, that tragedy is a genre, encompassed by something general, or generic?

The first step is to locate tragedy, definitively, within the text, more specifically the printed text on the page. Where Eagleton wants to unmoor the term 'tragedy' from (mere) aesthetic considerations, what is really required is to make an aesthetic consideration of tragedy matter to readers today. The tragic effect is not to be recovered by immersing ourselves in a world elsewhere, historical or otherwise, or more deeply in the immediate social, political or ecological disasters of the present. The claim that tragedy does not exist today speaks not to the fact that tragedies are no longer being written, but to the fact that they are no longer being read, or *felt*. The Holocaust may or may not be 'tragic'; such a debate is beyond the scope of this study. The more salient critical question is, faced with horrors like the Holocaust, should we care to read about the tragic fate of a Danish prince?

That tragedy, whatever it is, exists outside of, or operates beyond, perfect human understanding is perhaps no lesson we should impart to others, particularly if we take the
goal of any critical endeavour to be greater understanding.
But one cannot begin with an understanding of helplessness;
one must *discover* one's helplessness. The trajectory is not of
moving from limitlessness to suitable limits; rather, beginning with limits, we must discover limitlessness. The limits to
begin with are located in the play, or written speech; the discovery of limitlessness, squarely in the reader imagination.
It is in the oscillation between a consideration of limits and
limitlessness (the play immediately before us versus counterfactual reader responses to that play) that the tragic effect
resides.

Counterfactual speculation is a type of reader response
which presupposes that the tragic effect can be felt, which
is to say articulated, outside of (1) the historical contingencies that first led to the production of the work in question
and (2) direct reference to immediate historical realities the
reader, interpreter or viewer now finds himself or herself in.
Not that reference to (1) or (2) is to be avoided outright.
But the principal limiting factor of any discussion of tragedy will be the play itself and not the society that bred it. In
moving towards limitlessness, rather than grounding critical
discussions of tragedy in facts and figures taken from the
world beyond the immediate experience of the text, what
this project proposes is multiplying and analysing some of
the countless number of narrative contingencies suggested
within the play, prioritising these over the myriad contingencies no doubt available without.

According to Cavell, speech is surely more 'present' to
us when spoken in the present, in our presence, as on stage.
How to square his emphasis on speech with an emphasis on
counterfactual *reading*, rather than viewing? No doubt a play
being performed has as much opportunity to elicit thoughts

about how else a performance *could have* been staged, based not only on language (delivery), but on costume and set-design, for example. Yet the move into the subjective realm of possibility is the sort that haunts our psychic, rather than immediate physical, existence. Here it seems, once again, that the critical enterprise to follow entails a move away from what is immediately present to the senses. Yet to insist on attending to speech rather than props is to attempt to limit ourselves to spoken language in the consideration of pos-sibilities. That spoken language can appear on paper as well as on stage carries one immediate ramification. On stage, not only are the time and metre of the language imposed on us, but so too is the time it takes for the play to unfold. When reading a play, we have more opportunity to break free from the intrusion of time – to go back over lines, pages, scenes – to attend to lost possibilities. So while actors can make a claim to be in our present, what we want, in a way, is to increase our ability to be in their (the characters', and not the actors') present. The ability to do so is not *negated* when watching a play. There are all sorts of ways a given actor's interpreta-tion of lines can point to, enhance, or leave something to be desired from, the suggestiveness of certain lines. But, as Cavell reminds us, it remains a fact that as far as actors on a stage are concerned, they are 'in our presence',[41] though we are not in theirs. We could entertain breaking down the so-called 'fourth wall' in hopes of achieving the type of pres-entness we desire. Indeed, this has something to do with the sorts of effects Antonin Artaud and Bertolt Brecht have in mind in proposing their particular alterations of theatrical convention (more in Chapter 3). However, a break from the external time imposed on the play when reading the play (in private) is a boon to counterfactual thinking.

Nonetheless, speech does carry its own rhythms. Estab-lishing the limit as the play itself is not to emphasise reading *new lines* into the play, because to do so would be to betray the particular rhythms that tune us into the present in the first place. Such rationale speaks to why pursuing counterfactuals is perhaps unsuited to reading novels. Novels chart out their own internal 'directedness' based on much more than merely the speech of their characters. To ask what if one thing had happened rather than another would be analogous to asking, in plays, what if one character had *said* one thing, or said the same thing in a different (e.g. prosy) way, rather than another. To ask what if Jeanie Deans had simply lied to save her sister (in Sir Walter Scott's *Heart of Midlothian* (1818)) would be to demolish the novel as a whole, or to presuppose an entirely different text. Furthermore, it would not be entirely clear, in pursuing counterfactuals in novels, whose presentness we would seek to be establishing intimacy with – the author's or the character's. Surely Scott is saying something about the world at large in describing the world he does as he does. Novelists, like theorists, present us with *a* subjectivity: their own. Shakespeare, on the other hand, working exclusively with speech, presents us with subjectivities. Part of unpacking a novel is to establish the author's worldview. We may try to do the same with Shakespeare, but his plays demand criticism of a different sort.

Going back to critiquing historicism, note how practitioners of the 'New' sort distinguish themselves from the 'Old'. Traditional historicists, like E.M.W. Tillyard, tied the goings on in any of Shakespeare's plays to an already existing 'Elizabethan world picture'. In contradistinction, Jean E. Howard wants

> to sketch what must of necessity be a simplified picture of some of the assumptions underlying the historical criticism of a figure such as Tillyard. These assumptions include the following: that history is knowable; that literature mirrors or at least by indirection reflects historical reality; and that historians and critics can see the facts of history objectively.

(This last assumption is particularly paradoxical since it rests on the premise that while literature is implicated in history, historians and critics are not.)[42]

For New Historicism to distinguish itself from the positivistic predilections of the Old, the historicist must now attempt to answer and deal effectively with these assumptions. The pertinent dichotomy to consider is whether a text (in the Renaissance or otherwise) works to entrench established meanings on the one hand, or create meanings and hence, by so doing, subvert, rather than prop up, existing social relations on the other. Indeed, Howard notes that Greenblatt's 'degree of methodological self-consciousness'[43] comes in his refusal to grant primacy to either side, with his New Historicist insistence that a text, while often buttressing social norms, does indeed carry subversive potential. Commenting on Greenblatt's obsession with identity formation and self-fashioning, Howard says

> [Greenblatt] seems to suggest that discourse about the self has no single point of origin but constantly evolves in response to various forms of cultural authority, manifesting itself both in literary paradigms and in the construction of actual lives. In short, by stressing that he wishes to 'investigate both the social presence to the world of the literary text and the social presence of the world in the literary text' ... Greenblatt moves to replace metaphors of mirrors and grounds with an interactive model of how the literary and the social texts relate.[44]

Yet in pursuing this methodology, however humane, it remains to be seen whether Greenblatt is not simply refashioning Old Historicist assumptions anyway. The first, 'that history is knowable', speaks to the second, which is whether or not a 'ground' of history can be established at all. Greenblatt seems to provide an answer by presupposing no stable ground of reference for the literary text, instead emphasising its existence in an in-between and circulatory space in which meanings are created. Yet what Greenblatt is doing *is* providing a 'ground', an objective ground, however liminal, allowing us to construct a stable and supra-historical space which we are to conceive of as the cradle of meaning. The problem is not in an insistence on creating a 'ground' per se, but in the assumption that *this* ground, or intermediate or interactive space, is itself not influenced by present conditions of discourse (the paradox Howard alludes to).

> In the work of Stephen Greenblatt one can find a somewhat different and more varied historical criticism ... but Greenblatt's recent writings also lead one, ultimately, to a consideration of the subversive or contestatory role which literature plays in culture. Up through his important book *Renaissance Self-Fashioning*, Greenblatt's main concern was identity formation. In that book he showed the historical moment defined the conditions of possibility for constituting selves in sixteenth-century England. In a series of careful analyses he examined how selves took shape in the sixteenth century in relationship to specific authorities and their culturally-derived antitheses or demonic others. Among the many influences on the book is Lacan's neo-Freudian psychology with its assumption, not of a unified and autonomous self, but of a provisional and contradictory self which is the product of discourse. Consequently, the book repudiates the humanist notion that man, the protean actor, is in control of his own identity formation; rather, he is presented in Greenblatt's work as the product of impersonal historical forces largely inimical to individual control.[45]

The heavy irony of this passage, not called out by Howard but, indeed, begging to be, is that Greenblatt himself exists within, is the product of, impersonal historical forces and influences (Lacan) that allow his particular methodology to resonate. All criticism, historical or otherwise, is itself a refashioning and can itself be interpreted as a response to existing power relations.[46] The idea behind using counterfactuals is to deny the need for objective space through the proliferation of subjective experiences of the text based not on a consideration of our historically determined presence to a text, but on our presentness within the text.

Of course, after the fact, the historian will come along to weigh in on just why such counterfactual questions were posed, why *these* counterfactuals resonated (and not others), and certainly there will be historical reasons why. This project starts with the assumption that however valuable such post-facto commentary may or may not be, it is of no relevance to the literary critic, whose job is to read the text at hand rather than document how it came to mean what it does. Literary critics, if they allow themselves to move beyond the historicist method, are in the position of *making meaning*. The historian, in his or her effort to create meaning, can only comment on how meaning is made. Striving for a supra-historical and objective view of the world, the historian not only passes up the opportunity to create meaning, but also actively, if unintentionally, works to quash any new meanings. New meanings always come from elsewhere, are methodologically 'knowable', reflect less on our present-day and historically contingent needs and more on a supra-historical past necessity and thus a knowable future. But is the future ever knowable? Why past necessity should take precedence over present-day needs is not entirely clear, particularly if we believe, as does Louis Montrose, that all modes of writing proceed 'from our own historically, socially and institutionally shaped vantage points'[47] situated first and foremost in the present.

Furthermore, the desire to locate Shakespeare on a trajectory of thought or thinking (historical or otherwise) is ultimately an attempt to make Shakespeare *verifiable*. The goal is not to read Shakespeare, but rather, to read him against a preconceived propositional backdrop that allows us, in a sense, to know the answers we are looking for before discovering them. This is to practice a type of critical 'formalism' the New Historicists sought to distance themselves from explicitly. Here Neema Parvini, discussing the work of prominent New Historicist Jonathan Goldberg, locates the principal tension not between New and Old Historicisms but between New Historicism and the formalism of the New Critics.

> [T]he fundamental organising principle for the formalist (whether a New Critic or a structuralist) is the text itself, [where] the organising principle for Goldberg is the text of 'culture'. He takes on board fully the post-structuralist notion that texts and contexts are inseparable and pushes it to its logical conclusion. But in doing so, 'culture' becomes the ultimate formalist text. Goldberg is guilty of reading 'culture' in precisely the way that the New Critics he opposes read literary texts.[48]

The New Historicists opposed the formal categories applied to Shakespeare a priori and the presupposition that the text *is* stable, presuppositions which indubitably led to the same readings. According to the New Historicists, Shakespeare, dressed in formalism, reaffirms the lessons of human nature known at the outset. What the New Historicists sought to do, in veritable post-structuralist fashion, was to deny any stable reference point from which Shakespeare could possibly mean. They highlighted the value of historical contingency and context as essential supplements to any understanding of meaning. Universal and ultimately non-linear interpretations of Shakespeare were radically undercut. Yet in time,

New Historicism came to look as 'formalist' as the criticisms it opposed:

> What's the difference between Tillyard saying that every Elizabethan believed in the Great Chain of Being and then seeing it everywhere in Shakespeare's plays and Green-blatt 'transcoding' ideologies from one 'discursive field' to another, from [historical] anecdotes to Shakespeare's plays?[49]

How did this happen? How did a methodology with so much promise and critical energy succumb to the formalist dragons it originally sought to slay?

In short, all propositional 'theories' applied to Shake-speare after the fact (whether Old *or* New Historicisms) require verification from beyond the text (New Critics, simi-larly reach(ed) for form over content). However much criti-cal energy such theories manage to mobilise at the outset, they will, of necessity, become conventional. New Histori-cism is not a 'hidden formalism',[50] as Parvini contends, as much as it *became a hidden formalism over time.*

Cultural materialists, on the other hand, do not delude themselves as to why Shakespeare means. They understand that the application of 'discursive fields' to Shakespeare speaks nothing of Shakespeare's timelessness or universal-ity, though these critics do favour, or seek to establish, the primacy of their particular vantage points, superior only because they acknowledge their situatedness in the present rather than make false claims of supra-historical objectivity. Here is Kiernan Ryan on the disjuncture between cultural materialists and New Historicists:

> The summons to pursue a *materialist* critique of culture, as opposed to establishing a cultural *poetics*, speaks volumes about the differences between these two styles of radical

criticism … Cultural materialism seeks actively and explicitly to use the literature of yesterday to change the world
today.[51]

While laudable in its acknowledgement of present-day contingencies, cultural materialism ends up subordinating Shakespeare to prevailing political needs, as though Shakespeare,
in order to be useful, meaningful, must necessarily footnote
discussion on identity politics.

Embarrassment, even anxiety, that the text *exists*, that it
itself is a capable progenitor of meaning, remains. Why are
we so anxious? Do we believe, if allowed, or if we let down
our guard, that Shakespeare is *destined* to result in readings
that further codify and entrench old oppressions? Arming
ourselves with justice at the outset presupposes that Shakespeare, left open to discovery, could *only* draw out from us,
hence act as a tool in the service of, hegemonic discourses of
injustice. Yet if we truly want to say that Shakespeare's texts
have the power of subversion, that his tragedies themselves
(and not the theoretical trappings they are dressed in) are
truly 'radical', then the only methodology we can bring to
Shakespeare in advance is a minimal one. The most profitable way forward entails discovering the precise nature of
our oppressions by attending to *the ways we read*. What cultural materialism would have us commit to instead is a suitable, ready-made and immediately applicable taxonomy to
be applied to Shakespeare in advance, ensuring we read him
correctly in the hope of guaranteeing our ability to sidestep
injustice for all time. Yet to read texts honestly and forth-
rightly is to risk self-exposure and discovery of our own
biases and injustices when reading. All that can be known in
advance is the existence of absences. In what sense are these
absences always-already there? In fact, they are not, until
language claims them, which is to claim ourselves and whatever it is we hold dear in our hearts, to our delight or dismay.

Simon Palfrey more readily appreciates the importance of letting Shakespeare lead our imaginations rather than having him chase other pieces of knowledge established a priori. Here Palfrey is talking not about possibilities in tragedy, but of those latent in the entire Shakespearean corpus.

> What is more, a formal economy such as Shakespeare's means that each instant, each expressive unit, remains definitively unfinished. Every last unit of speech lurks immanently in every single moment of the play, liable to be sparked into connection at any point. Words are not trapped in the action of their utterance, as though each word is an indivisible atom, cast upon the void. Each substantial word or phrase is animate with connections and confluences, which in turn move forwards and backwards into further relations; they supplement or modify what has been, and can be supplemented and modified in their turn, both by what has been and what is yet to come. We thus have to allow words both an achieved and a potential energy. They can be understood as still active in a kind of battle as to what they might mean, or waiting to be newly discharged into commission. Meanings can come true unevenly, quite outside punctual succession – which comes to seem a paltry way of measuring events, static and fossilizing. Things arrive, are even born, as though for the first time, in repeat performances or private readings. This means, in the most basic sense, that the history in the language is, from its very conception, anachronous, overlaying or latent with different times, events, possibilities.[52]

Yet this abundance of significance is not only daunting, but unmanageable. What counterfactual thinking provides is a minimal shape and grounding to Palfrey's intuition (providing it with suitable tuitions) by first reducing our scope to Shakespeare's tragedies and then focusing on the speech of his characters exclusively.

In concluding, let us return to Eagleton. Should we indeed be moving away from 'aesthetic' criticism and more towards what he might call 'social' criticism? If we already have enough historical material on which to 'ground' a discussion of tragedy, why insist on reading (rereading) Shakespearean tragedy, or tragic texts at all? Isn't the Holocaust tragic enough? I would argue that the value of pursuing strictly aesthetic concerns over the social is to avoid immediate 'interested' readings ultimately rooted in a consideration of power relations *for the time being*. In this way we place ourselves in a disinterested aesthetic atmosphere where an honest consideration of events and non-events does not carry immediate social and political repercussions. Once again, it is of no value to assume we know our politics in advance. We must discover our politics. Such is the value of turning to the written texts, concomitant with academic study.

Of course, some will say that no reading can ever hope to be completely disinterested, or carried out entirely outside of present-day conditions. It is the locale of such 'interest' that counterfactual thinking hopes to shift. The only way to speak outside of so-called 'objective' social forces is to increase subjective claims about a text. A 'reading', counterfactual or otherwise, cannot hope to be prescriptive. Rather, counterfactual thinking is merely an invitation to the reader to pursue a minimal 'methodology' in which significance (because everything that didn't happen is now possible) has to be created. More precisely, the discovery or meaning to be made is one that occurs after a convincing subjective consideration of limitlessness from within some manner of acknowledged limits. The usual trajectory of post-structuralist inquiry is the reverse; we begin knowing that nothing means, only to (1) reiterate the fact of meaninglessness, or (2) commit to minimal limits designed as stand-ins for a lack of meaning, as 'last words' on the text. But reality does not end *there*, limited thus; rather, reality *is* limitless; how we impose limits on that reality, how we reason our way out of limitlessness, is a critical task that could only be generative, not definitive. We can always revisit texts and only in revisiting texts anew are we open to tragedy.

One final quotation from Howard on the value of reading, rather than explaining (historically), a text:

> A good reading can be a masterpiece, but it usually has the status of an isolated event. Essays which explain how and why one does and should read in a particular way are both more generous and more risky since they do not try to seal themselves off from what is polemical by aspiring to a timeless commonsense, but expose what is difficult and what is at stake in 'making knowledge' at this historical moment.[53]

The value of historicist inquiry is that it *does* seek to explain why or how we read a certain way. Close readings, on the other hand (according to Howard), in their appeal to 'timeless commonsense' without foregrounding their historical assumptions, are less generous simply because they refuse to engage with the stakes or analyse the implications of their presumptions. But close readings themselves can be a form of generosity. How generous is it to present a definitive way to read a text simply to be imitated, or a taxonomy simply to be applied, particularly if reader subjectivity is quashed? Is this then to suggest that a reader who manages to express a subjective relationship to a text through close reading is, by default, appealing to a timeless common sense?

What such a reader is doing is creating, or refiguring, what we ought to take *to be* commonsensical, which is not timeless, but addresses a need for a particular significance at a particular moment in time. A certain critical generosity is necessary to accept a multitude of so-called isolated events. This doesn't mean that assumptions ought not to be called into question and analysed. Such an endeavour, however, has less to do with 'making knowledge' and more to do with making knowledge uniform. The tension, perhaps, is healthy. But to overemphasise, continually, our inability to get outside language games is not a stance of critical generosity, but of critical patrimony. If meaning is made in isolated events, we need more of these events, not fewer. Nor does this exclude a consideration of stakes.

The stakes are best addressed by looking at another text of Nietzsche's, one that does not mention tragedy explicitly but which carries implications for the project at hand. In his *On the Advantage and Disadvantage of History for Life*, Nietzsche advocates a historical forgetting for the sake of life. His emphasis, however, is not on a total disavowal of history but on reclaiming the value of what he calls the 'unhistorical condition'.[54]

> It [the 'unhistorical condition'] is the most unjust condition in the world, narrow, ungrateful to the past, blind to dangers, deaf to warnings, a little living whirlpool in a dead sea of night and forgetting: and yet this condition – unhistorical, contra-historical through and through – is the cradle not only of an unjust, but rather of every just deed; and no artist will paint his picture, no general achieve victory nor any people its freedom without first having desired and striven for it in such an unhistorical condition. As the man of action ... is always without conscience, so he is also without knowledge; he forgets a great deal to do one thing, he is unjust to what lies behind him and knows only one right, the right of that which is to become.[55]

Nietzsche does not say that any action beneficial to life must never look to history. He says that more often than not, a present action comes first, in unhistorical conditions, to which historical explanations are later tied. To assume that one can know, beforehand, what is just and what not, or what is tragic or what not, is to seek out knowledge disadvantageous to life.

Of course, one can get carried away with this rhetoric. Speaking strictly in terms of critical acts here, what are some of the ramifications of Nietzsche's thoughts? Where the tragic effect is located in Apollo's realisation that he 'could not live without Dionysus'[56] in *The Birth of Tragedy*, tragedy here can be linked homologously to the idea that whatever historical methods we use to explain the tragic effect, none is more powerful than an understanding that *the historical requires the unhistorical*. In making our case for the unhistorical consideration of possibilities, we next run into a consideration of limits. If everything now possible is open to critical scrutiny, how does this serve a condition of the unhistorical, particularly when, as Nietzsche says, forgetting is contingent on establishing limits, not limitlessness – what he calls 'horizon[s]'?

> And this is a general law: every living thing can become healthy, strong and fruitful only within a horizon; if it is incapable of drawing a horizon around itself or, on the other hand, too selfish to restrict its vision to the limits of a horizon drawn by another, it will wither away feebly or overhastily to its early demise. Cheerfulness, clear conscience, the carefree deed, faith in the future ... [each] depends on one's being able to forget at the right time as well as to remember at the right time; on discerning with strong instinctual feelings when there is need to experience historically and when unhistorically.[57]

The horizon this project proposes, mentioned previously, is the play itself, or written speech. Readers are to imagine not alternative voices, or speech, but alternative *events*. Speech remains constant, so to speak. Nietzsche notes that 'the animal, which is quite unhistorical and lives within a horizon ... nevertheless is in a certain sense happy, or at least lives without boredom and dissimulation'. Part of the urgency in pursuing counterfactual readings is to make Shakespeare, for pedagogical reasons, *less boring*, to increase the value of the text by divorcing it from the a priori buttressing of historical truths of a time gone by. Only when students are allowed to make the plays relevant to a subjective response in the present will they have the stamina and desire to go digging through the past. In this way counterfactual criticism is open-ended, generous and not definitive. Nor does it exclude other methods of inquiry (say, historicism), but rather anchors their discussions first and foremost to a present experience which must first be articulated in the present. Singular appeals to other subjective responses or mediations of a time gone by are not an explanation of tragedy, but an avoidance of the present. Once historical assumptions are made thus, present assumptions are invalidated, disparaged, or thought to exist merely as an extension of the past. Counterfactual thinking (particularly in the classroom, and particularly vis-á-vis tragedy) is a departure point only – is, in a way, *the* departure point. Whatever we discover about the past only makes sense, is meaningful, as an extension of a response made and acknowledged in the present. So what students require is the space to tease out possibilities in texts without immediately attending to historical data. Shakespeare, more specifically Shakespearean tragedy, which elicits subjunctive longings, is as good a place to start as any in initiating some version of the examined life.

The counterfactual readings which follow have been arranged for the sake of argumentation. Each chapter builds upon knowledge discovered previously, so it may be difficult to follow my train of thought by reading each chapter on its own. The 'proof' of the method comes in the strength of the discoveries or insights brought to bear, and I am happy for the reader to judge whether, indeed, such insights are worth bringing to bear. This project, while wanting to establish the worth of counterfactual thinking, in addition, or perhaps simultaneously, provides a critique of thinking propositionally, or 'dialectically', particularly in relation to reader reception of tragedy. Whether or not this project provides an effective critique is something I also invite the reader to consider.

In Chapter 2, I discuss and juxtapose a reader desire for verification with necessity in *Hamlet*. The Ghost's story is a propositional utterance subject to the law of excluded middle (the story is either true or false). It can be, has the potential to be, verified. Our only verification of the Ghost's story comes via Claudius's confession, however. Without it, our ability to interpret Hamlet's delay, in particular our need to establish a thematic necessity for its occurrence via plausible post-facto explanation, is severely compromised.

Hamlet leads into a discussion of *King Lear*, which provides occasion for me to refine my reading of Cavell, particularly his understanding of the 'contingent' and the 'necessary' in the unfolding of tragedy. Whereas my discussion of *Hamlet* warrants a discussion of verification and necessity, the juxtaposition here of 'necessity' and 'contingency' reorients our narrative expectations. What *Hamlet* tempts us with is possible verification (of the Ghost's story). What *Lear*, and tragedy more generally, braces us for is the rapid unfolding of contingency. Knowing as we do how things are to turn out in *Lear*, it becomes virtually impossible to imagine the possible evil of Cordelia's initial transgression, and the possible (reader perception of) Regan and Goneril's sincerity in Acts 1 and 2. To put it counterfactually: what if we could disown our knowledge of *King Lear* before reading *King Lear*? What possible interpretive avenues are restored to our imagination?

Reader drive for propositional verification is put to the test in *Macbeth*, elucidated briefly in Hegelian terms in Chapter 4. Hegel seeks to describe a tragic fate. The post-facto discussion of tragedy requires telling the story of how one version of the tragic character came to be, necessitating the complete annihilation of any other. At first glance, and from a position of hindsight, the prophecy in *Macbeth* does seem to preclude the possibility of Macbeth not killing Duncan. As an external contingency imposed on the play, the prophecy manifests, of absolute necessity, what is taken to be Macbeth's tragic trait (ambition). Macbeth seemingly has no choice in the matter. We read *Macbeth* not to see whether the prophecy will play out, but how it will play out. Yet to read counterfactually is to assume, or take pains to establish, the primacy of the contingent over the necessary, which is to consider the possibility that Macbeth could have acted other than he did, despite even the existence of a prophecy that seems to suggest otherwise. I will isolate and discuss in greater detail the critical stakes involved in establishing the possibility of Macbeth's freedom over the elucidation of a tragic fate.

My reading of *The Winter's Tale* in Chapter 5 offers a sustained critique of Hegel's account of dialectical unfolding. Because Leontes manages to survive a disastrous unfolding of events with his life intact, *The Winter's Tale* allows us to imagine life after tragedy's occurrence. What Leontes's 'post-tragic'[58] suffering uncovers or reveals is not that the occurrence of tragedy *necessitates* suffering, but that somehow, suffering is necessary to ennoble tragedy's occurrence – in a way to make peace with its occurrence. The counterfactual question to pose here concerns how we read not Hermione's miraculous resurrection, but rather, Leontes's equally miraculous conversion and acceptance of the oracle's truth in Act 3. What if, even after all is said and done, the oracle is incorrect? Can we entertain the *possibility*? Certainly Leontes does. In fact, his subsequent acceptance of the oracle is not a matter of necessity at all, but is, like Edmund's conversion in *King Lear*, an act of radical contingency. It need not have happened, an insight which exposes our remarkable vulnerability in explaining why or how it does happen.

Finally, in my reading of *Othello*, I argue that to seek out eternally something like verification, truth or falsity, introduces into our thinking a type of dialectical sickness. If all things are possible not at all times, but over an infinite amount of time, then the opportunity to defer tragedy and its horror exists endlessly. To defer tragedy in this way is essentially to marginalise its potency in human affairs, which could be a psychically liberating manoeuvre. We do not think of Iago as tragic, for example, precisely because he makes such a manoeuvre. He is immune to tragedy because he is immune to the power of words, perpetually deferring their meaning. His Machiavellianism allows him to live to fight another day, and all of us want this sort of power, Othello included. However, where Othello wants to be impervious to tragedy (like Iago), he is unable to divorce himself from the potency of (his own) words (unlike Iago).

In my conclusion, I make the case that to do counterfactual criticism is to 'suffer' criticism. One way the characters in the plays are made to suffer is in their unknowing of how things are at present, and, of course, how things are to turn out in future. Critics, analogously, must forgo the search for propositional truth verifiable over time when reading tragedy and be willing to embrace a fair amount of anxiety in unknowing precisely where counterfactual criticism will take us.

CHAPTER 2

MY KINGDOM FOR A GHOST:
COUNTERFACTUAL THINKING AND *HAMLET*

A.C. Bradley's use of character criticism as a means of explaining tragedy away is not a pitfall he is insensitive to. Bradley recognises that the very act of explaining risks explaining (something like tragedy) away.

> Any answer we give to the question [of the source of tragic power] … ought to correspond with, or to represent in terms of the understanding, our imaginative and emotional experience in reading the tragedies. We have, of course, to do our best by study and effort to make this experience true to Shakespeare; but, that done to the best of our ability, the experience is the matter to be interpreted, and the test by which the interpretation must be tried. But it is extremely hard to make out exactly what this experience is, because, in the very effort to make it out, our reflecting mind, full of everyday ideas, is always tending to transform it by the application of these ideas, and so to elicit a result which, instead of representing the fact, conventionalizes it. And the consequence is not only mistaken theories; it is that many a man will declare that he feels in reading a tragedy what he never really felt, while he fails to recognize what he actually did feel. It is not likely that we shall escape all these dangers in our effort to find an answer to the question regarding the tragic world and the ultimate power in it.[1]

Why should conventionalising Shakespeare's tragedies be more of a threat today than when Bradley wrote in 1904, enough of a threat to warrant radically different interpretive approaches? One reason is that the historicist method entails the types of misperceptions that Bradley alludes to: a replacement of feeling with explanation and, in time, convention. However unlikely it may be that interpretation can avoid conventionalising the tragic effect, Bradley is sympathetic to critical efforts attempting as much. Yet he, or at least the manner in which his brand of character criticism has been taken up, also consigns us to searching for conventional prescriptive answers, if not in the immediate historical contingencies of Elizabethan England, then in definitive character traits, known in tragedy as 'flaws'.

Certainly Bradley perceives the tragic effect, comprehends its mystery as being open-ended. But why insist on isolating a tragic flaw at all? This virtually guarantees that we will, in fact, conventionalise the mystery of tragedy through character interpretation. The explicit question to be taken up in this chapter concerns Hamlet's delay – that is, how to read it? In addressing the question, I will show how the need to read it as problematic, which Bradley clearly does, conventionalises tragedy. In an attempt to achieve 'presentness', we must attend to our first responses to the play, which means attending to the possibility that we would, without prior knowledge, perceive the delay as something relatively unproblematic. We are discussing the possibility not of competing Hamlets, but of competing readers of *Hamlet*.

What are some possible first responses worth attending to? Bradley notes two:

> Suppose you were to describe the plot of *Hamlet* to a person quite ignorant of the play, and suppose you were careful to tell your hearer nothing about Hamlet's character, what impression would your sketch make on him? Would

he not exclaim: 'What a sensational story! Why, here are some eight violent deaths, not to speak of adultery, a ghost, a mad woman, and a fight in a grave! If I did not know that the play was Shakespeare's, I should have thought it must have been one of those early tragedies of blood and horror from which he is said to have redeemed the stage'? And would he not then go on to ask: 'But why in the world did not Hamlet obey the Ghost at once, and so save seven of those eight lives?'[2]

In fact, what Bradley is highlighting is not a possible first reaction to the play, but to a later summarisation. The play has been reduced through post-facto description in a way that presupposes the delay as a problem a priori. But Bradley goes on to note that in the first instance, the above reaction is not likely to be felt:

The exclamation [that Hamlet should have killed the king instantly] and this question both show the same thing, that the whole story turns upon the peculiar character of the hero. For without this character the story would appear sensational and horrible; and yet the actual *Hamlet* is very far from being so...

We are all aware of this, and if we were not so the history of *Hamlet*, as a stageplay, might bring the fact home to us. It is ... the most popular of Shakespeare's tragedies on our stage; and yet a large number, perhaps even the majority of the spectators, though they may feel some mysterious attraction in the hero, certainly do not question themselves about his character or the cause of his delay, and would still find the play exceptionally effective, even if he were an ordinary brave young man and the obstacles in his path were purely external. And this has probably always been the case. *Hamlet* seems from the first to have been a favourite play; but until late in the eighteenth century, I believe, scarcely a critic showed that he perceived anything specially interesting in the character.[3]

If it was 'probably always ... the case' prior to the late eighteenth century that Hamlet's delay was not perceived as particularly problematic, it is difficult to understand why Bradley turns to the question of Hamlet's character so explicitly. How, that is, do we go from not noticing the delay to exclaiming, as Bradley's hypothetical reader does, that Hamlet *should have* killed the king? Where, when or how does the delay gain the normative hold it does – or where, when and how does a certain brand of criticism arise that focuses on Hamlet's character? Why should the whole story suddenly turn on the question of the hero? When Bradley later says that 'whatever we ... may think about Hamlet's duty, we are meant in the play to assume that he *ought* to have obeyed the Ghost', he is making a claim with the benefit of hindsight.[4] It only becomes apparent that Hamlet ought to have obeyed the Ghost when everything ends so poorly. Had the play ended happily, we would have no normative claim on Hamlet. In short, Bradley is well on his way to making the delay a problem a priori without consulting posterior experience of the play. If the play is or once was intelligible without calling attention to the delay, then it is not necessarily true that we would (1) ask why Hamlet had not obeyed the Ghost right away and (2) assume that Hamlet ought to have obeyed the Ghost at all. It is perfectly reasonable, upon first reading or viewing, to go along with Hamlet's doubts, to demand as he does verification of the Ghost's testimony, to wonder whether the Ghost is a 'spirit of health or goblin damned' (1.4.21).

I note here a distinction between verification and necessity. Verification occurs within the unfolding of the play. Necessity, on the other hand, occurs outside or beyond the play and is established by acts of criticism after the fact. Only we as readers require necessity; Hamlet has not the luxury of demanding it. He merely requires that the Ghost's testimony be verified, and we are happy to go along with him as he

seeks verification. However, we (and in hindsight) addition-
ally require that the delay *make sense* – that it attest to *something*, either thematic about *Hamlet* or about the character
Hamlet, that is *necessary*. The mix-up occurs as soon as we
hear Claudius's confession. At that point, we exit the realm
of verification. The problem of Claudius's guilt, for us, is
no longer *to be* verified; it *is* verified. But if it makes sense
to go along with Hamlet as he seeks verification, we cannot
suddenly begin to read the delay as problematic or establish
a critical necessity for it while Hamlet himself still seeks to
verify Claudius's guilt. (I will return to this point.) Surely,
Hamlet laments that he delays, but he never laments *his
delay*, the particular moment when he reneges on the opportunity to kill Claudius at prayer. That he wishes Claudius to
hell and not heaven may not be reason good enough for us.
But nowhere in the play is it suggested that this reason is particularly troubling to Hamlet. The real moral question is not
'why does Hamlet delay?' but 'what if we as readers had not
heard Claudius's confession?' How would we then read the
delay? As a moment pregnant in dramatic significance? Or as
a rather unremarkable occurrence consistent with Hamlet's
character that attests not to his weakness, but to the prudence and wisdom befitting a prince?

Yet even without Claudius's confession, we would still
have all sorts of instances calling attention to Hamlet's
procrastination – his 'coward[ice]' (2.2.548), his 'blunted
purpose' (3.4.101), his 'dull revenge' (4.4.9.23),[5] his tardi-
ness – enough, once the play is over, to make the case convincingly that Hamlet believes he ought to have done the
deed. It remains to be seen, at such a point, whether *we*
would concur. It is perfectly reasonable without Claudius's confession to read Hamlet as a character troubled by
his hesitations. But Hamlet's procrastination would not
become so palpable a problem for *us*. Without the confession, we would have no way of either endorsing or

condemning Hamlet's vacillations. We could not say he is wrong to vacillate, to say as convincingly as Bradley does that he ought to have killed the king. Yet we could not exactly say that he is right to vacillate because, in the end, he does the deed. So his vacillations are redeemed.

This asymmetry in knowledge between what we know about *Hamlet* from without and what Hamlet knows about goings on at court from within is touched upon, rather humorously, by René Girard:

> Why should a well-educated young man have second thoughts when it comes to killing a close relative who also happens to be the king of the land and the husband of his own mother? This is some enigma indeed, and the problem is not that a satisfactory answer has never been found but that we should keep looking for one. Should our enormous critical literature on *Hamlet* fall someday into the hands of people otherwise ignorant of our mores, they could not fail to conclude that our academic tribe must have been a savage breed, indeed.
>
> After four centuries of controversies, Hamlet's temporary reluctance to commit murder still looks so outlandish to us that more and more books are being written in an unsuccessful effort to solve that mystery. The only way to account for this curious body of literature is to suppose that back in the twentieth century no more was needed than the request of some ghost, and the average professor of literature would massacre his entire household without batting an eyelash.[6]

Girard is being facetious because we do know that the average professor of literature is not ready to accept that Hamlet *ought* to massacre his uncle or his household, at least not right away. Even if the average professor of literature believes that Hamlet is procrastinating, none will deny the relative sagacity and temperance behind Hamlet's desire to verify his intuition before taking any rash action. Up to (although perhaps not after) the dumb show and player scene, we are prepared to read Hamlet's doubts not as some symptom of sickness, but as indicative of a mind displaying some foresight and healthy scepticism. But once the king rises, once he has betrayed his guilt, surely *this* should be reason enough to remove both us and Hamlet from the realm of (seeking) verification. Both Hamlet and we readers now have all the verification required. Only the deed remains to be done. Surely at this point, we can agree with Bradley that Hamlet ought to obey the Ghost.

But how should Hamlet proceed? Hamlet cannot spring at the king's throat at just that instant. No matter; the king retires to his chambers. Soon enough, Hamlet has a terrific opportunity as he stumbles upon Claudius at prayer. Now armed with the certainty afforded us by the dumb show and player scene, we are indeed screaming for Hamlet to do the deed. But our perception of Hamlet's delay is tainted by the asymmetry in knowledge highlighted earlier. Do we know for a fact that Claudius is guilty? We do, but not because of the dumb show and player scene (which is all that Hamlet has to go on). Instead, we know by the fact that Claudius has just verified, for us exclusively, his guilt beyond a shadow of a doubt. Does Claudius's confession merely entrench something we know already, or is it the first instance in the play when we conclusively know that he is guilty? From the time that the king rises and before he confesses, how certain are we of his guilt?

Such concerns have been raised before. W.W. Greg's reading of the play throws enough ambiguity onto the events of the dumb show and player scene to challenge our certainty of the Ghost's existence. Greg points to the Ghost's testimony as a manifestation of 'Hamlet's hallucination'.[7] The easy rebuttal here is that Hamlet is not the only one who sees the Ghost; its appearance is confirmed by Horatio, Bernardo and

Marcellus, so it is not the coinage of Hamlet's brain alone. But Hamlet is the only one who *hears* the Ghost. This fact, coupled with the ambiguous turn of events during the dumb show and player scene, has Greg conclude that *the story* the Ghost tells Hamlet is a complete fabrication.

To recap briefly Greg's argument, let us remember that Hamlet's play-within-the-play in Act 3 is itself made up of two mini-productions. The first is the dumb show, in which anonymous characters act out a given argument. The second is the player scene (which Hamlet terms *The Mousetrap*), in which the player king (Gonzago) is murdered not by his brother but by his nephew (Lucianus) – a point reiterated explicitly by Hamlet to Claudius (3.2.216–23). In both productions, however, Hamlet has 'the actors play "something like" the murder of his father ... a minutely accurate representation of the whole story as told by the Ghost'.[8] So the king is *twice* faced with the representation of his crime in detail, yet rises only after the second. Greg writes:

> The King, it will be observed, gives not the smallest sign of disturbance during or after the all-important dumb-show ... any unprejudiced reading of the text will, I think, make it at once apparent that the only hypothesis consistent with the King's behaviour is that in the dumb-show he actually fails to recognize the representation of his own crime ... The manner in which the poison is administered makes even the shadow of a doubt absurd. There is but one rational conclusion: *Claudius did not murder his brother by pouring poison into his ears.*[9]

Moreover, it is not entirely clear to Greg that Claudius rises after the second poisoning:

> The supreme moment, so long anxiously expected, has arrived. The murderer empties his poison into the sleeper's

ears [for the second time], and – the King rises? Not a bit of it. Hamlet is unable to restrain himself any longer; he breaks out, hurling the crude facts of the story in the King's face, shouting, gesticulating, past reason and control. It seems as though the next moment he must sprint at his throat. Naturally the court breaks up, the King rises, calls for lights, and retires to his private apartments, convinced – not that his guilt has been discovered, but that Hamlet is a dangerous madman, who has designs on his life, and must, at all costs, be got quietly out of the country, and, if possible, out of the world.[10]

According to Greg, the king rises because he sees acted out before him the nephew of the Player King (and *not* a brother) committing regicide. Claudius sees not some past representation of a crime that he has committed, but the future possibility of his nephew taking his life. Claudius, not Hamlet Senior, is Gonzago, and Hamlet is, fittingly, Lucianus, 'nephew to the King' (3.2. 223).

Greg's argument is convincing, to say the least. The first counter to his claims is to reiterate that the king's initial non-reaction is hardly worth attending to because the Ghost's story is later verified by Claudius's confession. But if we are to imagine a version of *Hamlet* without the confession, we must ask whether there is enough ambiguity during the unfolding of events to make the forward progress of the play unintelligible. As Bradley noted, we are not likely to exit the realm of verisimilitude at any point during the play; it is largely effective. So is Greg's criticism of the play merely a criticism of hindsight, the sort that seeks to establish some narrative anomaly otherwise glossed over and to provide reasons for this anomaly? If we say that one is not likely to fuss that much over the anomaly during one's initial reading or viewing of the play, what has us *skip over* the fact that Claudius is indeed faced with the pantomime of a crime he supposedly committed?

A second counter to Greg, via Dover Wilson, is that it is obvious from the text that Claudius does not see the panto-mime. Ophelia nominates the dumb show as 'the argument' (1. 126). Claudius later asks in no uncertain terms: 'Have you heard the argument?' (1. 212), implying that he has not seen the dumb show. So we have textual evidence that Claudius was not attending to the argument of the play.[11] But when staging the play, this anomaly is more difficult to resolve. That is, how should Claudius be staged during the dumb show? For some, like Dover Wilson, the only way is to depict Claudius distracted while the poison is poured the first time. Claudius is frequently shown to be distracted while the dumb show unfolds despite the absence of explicit stage directions in the text. For others, this forced management of events without direction from the author is disconcert-ing.[12] To say that Greg's criticism of the play is only salient in hindsight denies the particular challenge of how to stage Claudius in the present. Greg's criticism could be vali-dated, rather than overlooked, simply by staging the play as directed. The equivalent in reading would be, perhaps, to pause after reading that the poison has been poured for the first time and wonder why Shakespeare does not have the king rise immediately.

The reason we largely do not has little to do with Claudius asking about the argument of the play. Eventually, he does rise – not necessarily to our satisfaction, but to Hamlet's. He seems convinced of the king's guilt when he says to Hora-tio, 'I'll take the Ghost's word for a thousand pound' (ll. 263–4). However much we may be confused by (gloss over) events upon reading the dumb show and player scene, Ham-let's reaction mediates our own. His conviction becomes our conviction; if he has all the evidence and corroboration he needs, why should we not follow along? So all that remains for him is to kill the king and follow through on the Ghost's imperative. The king retires before Hamlet can do so straight away. Next, we must consider how we would read his delay without the king's confession, armed only with Hamlet's conviction of the rightness of his cause. When the delay scene arrives, we have only Hamlet's conviction mediating our own. It is perfectly reasonable to assume that Hamlet's vacillation would mediate our response, that we would be quite willing to accept that, for whatever reason, killing Claudius in private would not be the best means to achieve any desired end. At the very least, we would no longer be wishing for Hamlet to do the deed. He has been 'delaying' in roughly the same manner throughout the play anyway.

Even if his delay is read as ratiocination, the key to our response would be in perceiving the justness or aptness of such ratiocination, in much the same way that we originally perceive the justness or aptness of putting Claudius to the test. This is why audiences prior to the late eighteenth century did not bother much with Hamlet's character or his delay. It is not because the five-act structure demanded a concluding bloodbath that Hamlet delays and then suddenly finds his resolve in the end. Instead, Hamlet 'delays' with perfect consistency of character throughout. How definitive is the king's reaction to the dumb show and player scene? Even if we say it is *absolutely* definitive for Hamlet, Greg shows us that we as readers would be wise to doubt it.

But then *how* exactly does the reaction become definitive for Hamlet? Why, in the rush of the present, should he and not we take the Ghost's word for a thousand pound? Surely that the king did not rise the first time passes before him *in exactly the same manner* as it does for us. Should Hamlet not have more reason to doubt? Is he, indeed, too caught up in the rush of the present to judge or read the king's actions correctly?

Of course, with the benefit of hindsight, and the benefit of Greg's reading, we can comfortably answer that he does get too caught up in the rush of the present – that Claudius's actions are not the smoking gun Hamlet craves. In fact, such a critical position – of highlighting Hamlet's rashness rather than his procrastination – could be quite commonplace in a counterfactual world of criticism without the confession. We must emphasise here that however we choose to view Hamlet at this juncture, as acting rashly or correctly, our answer can only be formulated in hindsight. In the rush of the present, it is equally possible to take the Ghost's word for a thousand pound (as Hamlet does) or to doubt the Ghost's story (as Greg does, supposedly in the present). Whether Hamlet or Greg is right or wrong is not the issue. The issue is not verification, which Hamlet seeks, but necessity, which Greg seeks to establish. Greg is interested in establishing that the Ghost is Hamlet's hallucination; hence, Greg must invalidate the Ghost's story in order to validate his reading of the play. For Greg, that Hamlet can be read as 'mad' makes the delay *necessary* and accounts for it. But armed only with a Ghost's story and a king who has risen after a second poisoning, can Hamlet be excused for jumping to conclusions? If you (like Greg) say 'no', then the other question indubitably follows: 'Can Hamlet be excused for *not* taking the Ghost's word for a thousand pound?' Whichever answer you choose does not invalidate the other because this is not a matter of fact and verification, but one of interpretation and (establishing) necessity. Does Hamlet interpret correctly? Without the confession, he does not, but with it, he does. Yet interpretation need not be *verified* to be useful. Whatever the case, with or without the confession, Hamlet could either have paused to make another stab at verification, or done just as he did. We as readers are at his mercy.

Moreover, Greg does not suggest that Hamlet remains in doubt; on the contrary, he assures us that Hamlet *is* certain that Claudius killed his father in the manner that the Ghost suggested. Greg, like Girard, *wants* Hamlet to doubt further, only, strangely, then to criticise him for it.

But what I want to emphasise here is that Hamlet (mis)per-
ceives, denies or overlooks the dumb show just as we do.
If we are capable of overlooking such an occurrence ourselves, then we can hardly separate ourselves from Hamlet
by saying that he knew incorrectly and that we somehow
knew correctly. We knew because Hamlet knew. But if we
are victims of Hamlet's (mis)interpretation of events, then
Hamlet is equally a victim. The events as they stand almost
beg us to reach for a conclusion (which only turns out to be
hasty in hindsight). The purpose of this exercise is to keep
our perceptions of events as close to Hamlet's as possible for
as long as possible. In my view, Hamlet is *no more certain* of
Claudius's guilt after the dumb show and player scene than
before. He behaves the same. It is we who are hasty, and not
because of the dumb show and player scene, but because of
the confession.

Yet Hamlet is not fated to do one *or* the other. It is perfectly reasonable to move in either direction, towards conviction in the rightness of one's cause or towards scepticism
about one's cause. The reason we move towards the former
upon first reading or viewing is because this is how Hamlet
instructs us to perceive the unfolding of events. After Hamlet
announces his conviction that the king is guilty, we are lucky
enough to stumble upon definitive verification. But audiences
in the past were not interested in or necessarily swayed by
such verification. Despite Claudius's confession, they were
willing to go along with Hamlet's vacillations because he is
all that has been mediating their understanding of events. In
a way, past audiences were far more *consistent* spectators of
the play.

Now, such glossing over can be a result of spectator lazi-
ness, so that to go along wholeheartedly with Hamlet's interpretation or perception of events reneges on the work of
actual criticism, which takes a second look at the unfolding of
events and problematises what ought to be problematised and

is glossed over in the rush of performance. Allying ourselves uncritically with the main protagonist's view of unfolding is not, perhaps, a fruitful critical strategy to pursue. But once we are given Claudius's confession and the time to ponder it in hindsight, we stake our claim as readers separate from Hamlet. As readers of the play, we occupy a privileged position of knowledge to which Hamlet does not have access. But this narrative fluke (of hearing Claudius confess) causes us to lose sight of how much we are indebted to Hamlet to chart out for us the appropriate response of a prince who suspects that something is rotten in the state of Denmark.[13] As soon as we leave the realm of contingency, we decry Hamlet for not acting fast enough (or perhaps for sullying the experiment by nominating himself the 'nephew' rather than the 'brother'), in the end turning his delay into a problem. But Hamlet, mortal soul that he is, must find the means and will to act within a world of contingency, a world lacking verification.

So is the Ghost a hallucination or isn't it? Is it right for Hamlet to act upon his intuition (ostensibly proved true by the figure of the Ghost) or to delay upon feeling it and then seek out verification? This is a matter of interpretation, and both possibilities remain open. The Ghost says A (Claudius murdered the king). Either A is true or it isn't. With Claudius's confession, A is most certainly true. But let us assume that A is or could be untrue – an assumption we indubitably hold the entire time of the play prior to Claudius's confession. What if the narrative of the Ghost *is* Hamlet's hallucination? Without the confession, we have no way of knowing that A is true. When the play ends, Claudius's *original* crime of regicide is not exposed to the court. Claudius is punished for his most immediate crimes only, including the inadvertent murder of his queen and Laertes and the murder of the crown prince. Horatio says he will tell Hamlet's story, but what exactly is that story? Will Horatio reveal that Hamlet and the others on the watch were visited by a Ghost? There is still no proof that Claudius killed the king. Establishing such a wild claim would only reduce Hamlet's posthumous standing at court, not bolster it. Why not leave Claudius punished for the very apparent crimes he has committed, instead of trying him for a crime based on nothing more than the testimony of a Ghost?

In a way, Claudius's original crime is beyond redress. No indication is given at play's end how the court will proceed, but if Horatio has any sense, he would be wise to put the Ghost story to bed. Moreover, without the confession, we – like Hamlet, and the court at the end of the play – would have no access to truth or to verification. So what are we left with? Un-truth? Surely we are left with something, perhaps the contingency of the unverified and the understanding that the truth cannot set us free because there is no reason to believe the truth is ever forthcoming – no reason to suggest that without the confession there is any way for the play to end to our satisfaction. So the question is not how Hamlet knows, but whether or not *we* know and, if we insist that we do, to ask ourselves how we know in contradistinction to how Hamlet knows.

Where does this leave us in terms of tragedy? We began with Bradley, who said that Hamlet's soul is sick, 'diseased' with melancholy.[14] Greg argues that Hamlet suffers from hallucinations. For him, that the Ghost is incorrect does not lead us to sympathise with Hamlet's vacillations; they lend credence to the understanding that Hamlet's original intuition of his uncle's treachery is founded upon nothing more than unhealthy psychological hang-ups resulting from the normal day-to-day repressions of 'feelings, memories, and almost instinctive beliefs'.[15] For Girard, the possibility that the Ghost is incorrect is never at issue. In Girard's reading, Hamlet's sickness is not some sign of prudence or foresight. Although there is a moral element to Hamlet's aversion to carrying out revenge, that he ultimately capitulates and does the deed is read by Girard not as an ending proper to the play, but as one that Shakespeare was forced to write as a means of appeasing the bloodlust of Elizabethan spectators. A proper ending, for Girard, would have been for Hamlet to keep on vacillating. The question of justice, of Claudius's ostensible guilt, is not discussed; Hamlet should have turned the other cheek. It is difficult to know whether the ending makes *Hamlet* failed tragedy for Girard (something more akin to spectacle), or whether the tragedy is that Hamlet forgoes his hesitation, committing the deed Girard would have him relinquish. But it is not the bloodbath of the final act that satisfies the audience's bloodlust; *it is Claudius's confession.* What kind of play would we have without the confession? If you say at such a point that the play would become unintelligible, would run its course unsatisfactorily, you are saying that something we demand has not been adequately fulfilled. What we demand is not the final bloodbath we get, *but the reason or rationale attesting to the justness of that bloodbath.*

Claudius's confession allows us to take a position of strength against Hamlet, to validate our distance from him, to enact revenge on him for not knowing what we have the privilege of knowing. Making the delay a problem, even implicitly as Girard does (he discusses the delay as an objective correlative attesting to the fact that Hamlet is indeed sick), validates the cycle of revenge. *We* are happy, satisfied, appeased, *knowing* Claudius is guilty. But no one else knows: no one at court and arguably not even Hamlet.

Hamlet is tragic because it charts out the terror of a world of contingency and half-knowledge, and how to justify oneself lacking knowledge, armed only with a hunch. The idea that sometimes one can know something but not (ever) have it verified invites philosophical speculation about what constitutes knowing. That there are limits to what we can know, even at the empirical level, is the sort of uncomfortable truism, even taboo, that *Hamlet* highlights. By 'taboo', I mean what cannot be expressed in either thought or language because certain a priori information blocks our ability to conceptualise it fully. The a priori knowledge we have once the play has ended is of Claudius's ostensible guilt. Our knowledge of his guilt blinds us to the likelihood that without the confession, we would have no way of making the play intelligible. The play would remain unresolved. Indeed, the ending we get puts Claudius's crimes beyond redress *absolutely*. If we were not privy to Claudius's confession, we would be left to fend for ourselves in a world of contingency, unable to hide from the fact that a perfect knowledge is beyond our grasp.

So what has any of this to do with the delay in particular? Are we not more concerned here with Claudius's confession than with Hamlet's delay? But the two are intimately linked. Our perception of the latter only becomes problematic after we hear the former. In order to speculate on how we might receive the play anterior to the knowledge that Hamlet's delay is an enigma or riddle to be solved, we must ask ourselves how we would read the delay without the preceding confession.

And why should such an exercise be useful at all? Any number of events could be negated, and in each of these instances we would have a different play with different ramifications. The work of criticism is to talk about the play we do have; engaging in these sorts of hypothetical narratives betrays or denies the possibility of explaining what is in all reality before us. But we are not advocating abandoning the text, but instead adopting a strategy that allows us to see it better. For instance, Claudius's confession is spoken to no one. Nothing he says elsewhere is negated or contradicted to the point where the play's coherence is compromised; removing the confession does not cause the play to unravel. The confession, as an event in the play, does not simply acquaint us with Claudius's subjectivity in the manner of a soliloquy or an aside. Claudius's confession serves a function that allows the narrative to progress. To imagine what sort of play we would have without it does not take us into some esoteric realm of counterfactual speculation that *no one* inhabits. It gives us access to the world of contingency that *all of the characters within the play are situated in immediately*. We are not more present to some other play and less present to this one. We are, in fact, more present to a world just adjacent to us on stage; in removing the confession, we do not flesh out alternative events per se, but uncover an alternative perception of the same events. By attending to our perceptions, rather than focusing solely on Hamlet's character, we shift the locale in which tragedy functions from something inner (which can be explained as 'necessity' or 'flaw') to something outer. And if the occurrence of outer events, including our perception of them, has more to do with contingency (something as contingent as the order in which events take place or happen to be perceived), then to emphasise the play of the contingent in the occurrence and reception of tragedy, one must consider not the necessity of outer events that do occur but the contingency of their occurrence. The only way to do this is not to assume that what happened *had* to happen the way it does, but to entertain other possibilities, in terms of both what happens to the characters in the story and our perception of those characters.

What such knowledge of contingency forefronts in the case of *Hamlet* is the possibility that we live in a world where perfect knowledge is not forthcoming and that conditions can exist in our finite perception of the world that put perfect knowledge beyond our grasp. And we are talking not about some sort of otherworldly or infinite knowledge, but about an absolute inability to access the knowledge we require to construct a meaningful notion of justice.[16] This is the taboo

Hamlet underscores – not how to move forward in a world lacking perfect knowledge, but how to exist in a world in which even finite knowledge is beyond reach. That flagrant crimes can go unpunished – nay, can go unknown – is almost too frightening a possibility to bear. Does it matter that Claudius killed the king if the state thrives afterwards?

What is immediately at stake in *Hamlet* is a certain type of knowledge – call it intuition – the sort that exists anterior to verification. How can we *know* something if it has yet to be verified? Is it a matter of honour that Hamlet is guided by his intuition or a matter of responsibility that he puts such unverifiable longings to rest? This is arguably what Hamlet tries to do with the play-within-the-play. Greg's reading forces us to ask whether Hamlet did indeed receive verification of any sort. Even if we conclude that he did not, how or why did he gain the conviction he did? And if we insist on *not* separating ourselves from Hamlet, if we insist on facing the present as Hamlet does, we can only conclude that to take the Ghost's word for a thousand pound or to doubt the Ghost as a hallucination are *both* equally valid interpretations, neither verifiable in the immediate present.

How to move forward armed only with intuition is a point taken up, albeit in a historicist register, by Carl Schmitt. According to Schmitt's reading of the play, Shakespeare achieves the stuff of high tragedy (as opposed to mere *Trauerspiel*) by allowing time – taken to mean real, historical time – to intrude on the play. By allying itself within and addressing a prevailing social taboo of Elizabethan and Jacobean England, *Hamlet* manages to elicit awe and wonder not because it gives vent to something its audience knows to be true but because it displays and thematises (while simultaneously protecting) something unventable, reaffirming the existence, however implicitly, of a taboo. This societal taboo is the one surrounding the dubious history of Mary Queen of Scots, mother of King James I:

> I can mention by name this wholly real taboo. It regards Queen Mary Stuart of Scotland. Her husband Henry Lord Darnley, James' father, was assassinated in a horrible way by the Earl of Bothwell in February 1566. In May, the same year, Mary Stuart married that very Earl of Bothwell, the murderer of her husband. Hardly three months after the assassination. Thus one may rightly talk of an unseemly and suspicious haste. To what extent had Mary Stuart taken part in the murder of her husband, or perhaps had been its instigator, that question has not been clearly answered to this day, and still remains controversial.[17]

James I inaugurated the reign of the house of Stuart, which only ended decisively after the overthrow of James II in 1688. According to Schmitt, the tragedy of *Hamlet* is lost once the taboo against the sovereign no longer commands power in the social imagination, and not because some new knowledge is unearthed, removing said taboo once and for all. Indeed, Schmitt reminds us that controversy surrounds Darnley's murder to this day. What Schmitt highlights is that in order to appreciate the high tragedy of *Hamlet*, the student of literature must immerse herself in the historical taboos surrounding the play's reception in Elizabethan England. This is not to prescribe, say, in traditional historicist register, immersion in what the elites of the time were discussing freely, but rather immersion in those discussions less blatantly in public circulation. But if historians today contend that Mary Queen of Scots was in fact guilty of murdering her husband, on what evidence can they stake their claim definitively? The sort that exists in absentia by virtue of its *non-appearance* in public discourse? In hindsight, the nature of this taboo is transformed. Where once it was taboo to discuss the possibility that King James's mother murdered her husband, what is difficult to face now is that we have not the means, may never be able to obtain the

means, to know definitively one way or the other. One reason the topic remains controversial is because it cannot be
put to rest. It risks exposing limits to our knowledge not
of the present, which is contingent, but of the past, which
(supposedly) is not. Nor, in such cases, is it simply a matter
of *interpreting* the past, as it is a given that interpretations
can change, are never verified definitively. In such cases, a
clear question is before us with zero-sum stakes. Either the
queen knew or she didn't. At stake is our ability to achieve
verification, without which we are in a limited position to
establish necessity or necessary post-facto interpretation of
any kind. So if this sort of taboo can never be resolved, what
does that entail? That we put our hunches or intuition about
Mary's guilt away?

> The taboo is perfectly explained by the time and the loca-
> tion of the composition of Shakespeare's *Hamlet*, and of
> its first performance between 1600 and 1603 in London.
> It was the time when everybody was awaiting the death of
> the old Queen Elizabeth of England, while her successor
> was still undecided. They were years of extreme tension
> and incertitude for the whole of England ... Nobody dared
> to talk about that delicate situation openly. An English-
> man who did talk had his hand cut off in punishment. The
> queen did not want to hear 'funeral tolls'. But under cover,
> everybody was talking and the various groups and parties
> were betting on different candidates.[18]

Schmitt is telling us that no one dared, openly, discuss the
succession of Queen Elizabeth. But in making one's case for
or against the accession of James VI of Scotland, one invari-
ably touched upon and discussed, however covertly, the possible murder of James's father by his mother. Only when
James finally ascended the throne was such a taboo removed
and the possibility of openly discussing his legitimacy put

beyond reach; verifying something many knew (suspected) to be true was no longer *possible*. Whatever one thought of Mary, one was not likely to gain traction moving forward on any indictment of the king's mother, especially when her son had come to terms with it. James I's ascension, in a sense, erased or denied a certain possibility of thought or thinking at the time. Even if Mary's treachery were true, even if she somehow could have confessed, her confession would be marred by 'those effects for which [she] did the murder' (3.3.54).

We need not historicise *Hamlet* to attune ourselves to Schmitt's reading. We can simply engage in counterfactual speculation. That is, without Claudius's confession, we are in the same position as James's subjects, unable to voice something we know to be true, that something *is* rotten in the state of Denmark. But how, if we are reading the play without the confession, do we know? If such is the case, we do not know. This fact touches on the particular relationship to knowledge that *Hamlet* thematises so succinctly, described by Eric P. Levy in his sympathetic reading of Hamlet's quest for a certain type of knowing:

> The problem of knowledge in *Hamlet* – the problem of 'things standing thus unknown' (5.2.350) – entails more than the intrinsic or constitutional inability of 'flesh and blood' (1.5.22) cognition to understand objects that by their very nature exceed its comprehension ... The fundamental epistemological problem in the play concerns, not the inherent deficiency of reason, but the disruptive effect of acquiring knowledge ... In *Hamlet*, the knowledge most urgently needed but most reluctantly acquired is *self-knowledge*. Ironically, Hamlet – the character whose motives remain obscure to others and who himself remains uncertain ... becomes the agent provoking painful self-knowledge in others.[19]

It is true that Hamlet seeks to account for his own suspicions in a dialectical fashion – he seeks to uncover truth in time to verify his intuition. But the fundamental problem, as Levy points out, is much deeper, for it is the nature of how one relates to an inner knowledge lacking outer verification (particularly when the inner knowledge in question has profound ramifications in the outer life of the state). Hamlet harbours a supposition about the world; yet the nature of his suspicions is an inner affair that requires inner verification made outer. The painful self-knowledge that Hamlet, the other characters, Elizabethans and even readers today are reluctant to face is not the possibility that power is capable of committing crimes beyond redress per se, but that conditions can exist that put a type of finite knowledge beyond reach eternally. So how indeed to move forward when something inner begs to become outer but, for whatever reason, cannot ever do so definitively?[20]

Such inquiry bears on how we read Hamlet's delay – as a problem that then entails asking how or whether we can once and for all resolve it. If we cannot now, do we simply wait for some definitive reading to spring up at some point in the future? But what if we commit to competing interpretations now? Just as no amount of historical truth can unearth whether Mary did or did not conspire to kill her husband, no amount of literary scholarship can ever hope to verify whether Hamlet was justified in his delay, simply because beyond the confession, which sets up an insurmountable asymmetry in knowledge (between us and Hamlet), we have no way of knowing – definitively, correctly, verifiably – that Claudius is guilty. No amount of research or thinking can ultimately unearth *the truth*. So what remains? An intuition and nothing more, with little definitive indication of whether Hamlet should act. We cannot say in hindsight that he *should have* – or, if we do, we must do so without benefit of the confession. But then, how tenuous would our normative

demand on Hamlet be? Can we say that he *shouldn't have*
and was right to delay? Both options remain open.

At the beginning of the play, Hamlet intuits rottenness, if
not in Denmark at large, then certainly at court. A father's
untimely death and a mother's hasty remarriage will do that.
With no real reason to doubt Hamlet's authority, we accept
it; hence, Hamlet's intuition (neither too hastily nor too ratio-
nally) becomes ours. But who else might have similar misgiv-
ings about the state? Let us not forget the voices of those
who also engage with, though do not speak to, what we take
to be the embodiment of Hamlet's suspicion, the Ghost. Let
us not forget the impressions of those on the watch:

> MARCELLUS. Good now, sit down, and tell me, he that
>   knows,
> Why this same strict and most observant watch
> So nightly toils the subject of the land,
> And why such daily cast of brazen cannon,
> And foreign mart for implements of war,
> Why such impress of shipwrights, whose sore task
> Does not divide the Sunday from the week:
> What might be toward that this sweaty haste
> Doth make the night joint-labourer with the day,
> Who is't that can inform me?   (1.1.69–78)

Those on the watch are witness to the militarisation of state.
Marcellus here expresses, if not outright opposition to such
militarisation, then at least anxieties about it. What does the
Ghost signify, if anything, to him? The Ghost signifies for
him, as it does for Hamlet, cause for suspicion. But Hamlet
is suspicious of his uncle while Marcellus is suspicious of
militarisation. Are the two related? More specifically, from
where does such suspicion originate? Are these ordinary
railings or extraordinary grievances? In fact, we have ample
evidence to suggest that both Hamlet's and Marcellus's

suspicions are misplaced or overblown. The coming war with Norway, for example, is deftly avoided by Claudius's diplomatic manoeuvrings. In Hamlet's case, it is less that the state is rotten than that Claudius himself is rotten. But then, my question becomes all the more relevant: does it matter *at all* that Claudius is corrupt if the state thrives afterwards? If rottenness can be contained, what business has Hamlet railing against his uncle, particularly if such railings risk the health of the state? In Marcellus's case, what is more salient: Claudius's deft handling of a direct military threat to Denmark, or his anxieties over the displacement (rather than the elimination) of violence (onto the Poles instead of the Danes)? These questions become political because what this play asks us to consider is who has the right, and when, *to rebel.* With the confession, certainly Hamlet and Marcellus have *the right*; but without it, how can we know? The strange placement, ambiguity and unfolding of events (the dumb show and player scene, the confession, and then the delay) bring this question to bear all the more forcefully. It is my claim that by focusing incessantly on the delay-as-problem, we deny the obvious question of justice that *Hamlet* forces us to consider. Only by considering the confession and delay as a single event are we faced with more urgent and uncomfortable truths: that power is capable of committing crimes beyond redress, and that the only way forward in such a scenario involves arming oneself with a type of knowledge – intuition – that attests not to something real, but to something *begging to become real.* This is not to ask if the Ghost is *merely* an intuition, but to ask whether the Ghost is a *useful* intuition, particularly if it paves the way for something like justice to be first *revealed* and only then, possibly, addressed. Why should we avoid discussions of justice anyway – how and in what way do they become taboo? Because such questions can never be put to rest, and risk exposing limits to our knowledge rather than our greater acquisition of it, it is far easier to assume we have all the verification we need in order to take heated stands and form well-wrought opinions over what is ultimately a non-issue. If the delay is irresolvable, it is not because of something we do not know now; it is because of something we can never know. The counterfactual thought experiment undertaken here has us see this clearly. The problem of the delay, ultimately, is only a problem at the centre, allowing us not to avoid a discussion of justice per se but to take its eventual manifestation for granted. Others at the periphery of court – like Hamlet, like Marcellus, and *like us without the confession* – must face, indeed must rail against, the terrifying possibility that the opportunity for redress has been missed, put beyond reach, *until death*. Sometimes, in the fight against injustice, a Ghost may be all we have.

CHAPTER 3

REVERSING GOOD AND EVIL: COUNTERFACTUAL THINKING AND *KING LEAR*

From a position of post-facto hindsight, Cordelia has to die in order for the tragic effect to take hold. To ask 'what if Cordelia had lived?' would be to erase *King Lear*'s tragedy. Yet Cordelia's death is not necessary within the world of the play. Indeed, Edmund's conversion in Act 5, his desire to take back the writ on her life, exposes the stark possibility of her living. Yet just as Hamlet's delay and Claudius's confession are linked, so too is Cordelia's death intimately related to our perception of Edmund's desire to take back the writ on her life. What if Edmund had not done so? The play, at least prima facie, would seem to make *more* sense. Shakespeare's insertion into the play of Edmund's change of heart risks the play's intelligibility. The question which follows is not necessarily why does she then die, or what sort of play would we have had Cordelia lived, but why would Shakespeare tempt us with the possibility of her living in the first place? To heighten the sense of devastation at the end?

As an act of radical contingency, seemingly arbitrary, Edmund's conversion seems to be placed in the play as a functional placeholder designed to elicit hope, only then to stifle it for the sake of greater tragic effect. Moreover, both Edmund's conversion and Cordelia's death can be 'explained' by appealing to something outside of the play itself – once again, to convention, or the conventions of tragedy. But such appeals counteract the power of these acts as contingent by anchoring them to something we can (only later) interpret as necessary. By an appeal to convention, the possible intelligibility of these acts within the world of the play is denied. Edmund's conversion becomes implausible at the very least, impossible at most. But Lear, having no access or appeal to convention, does not mourn the loss of his daughter any less. He must face the possible unintelligibility of her death, the gratuitous randomness of it.

Moreover, we don't know, or cannot conceive fully of, Cordelia's goodness until the play is over. This play is not like *Hamlet*, where we intuit some semblance of good and evil from the start and await verification. As quickly as we come to understand what we want verified by the narrative (Lear and Cordelia's standing redeemed, or verified as morally correct, at court, in some way), the possibility of this type of redress is just as quickly lost. If we want to say that Cordelia's goodness and her sisters' wickedness are evident after the love test alone, we must remember that the initial antagonism Shakespeare sets up in the play is not between Cordelia and her sisters, but between Cordelia and her father. At the level of subplot, we are given more adequate bearings. Shakespeare gives us plenty of motive for Edmund's treachery: his humiliation by his father for being a bastard is the play's opening scene. Initially, Edmund has no designs on the throne. He merely wants to dislodge Edgar from the inheritance of his lands.

None of the preceding statements are particularly insightful. However, by zeroing in our discussion of *Lear* around the contingency, rather than the necessity, of Edmund's conversion, we can read Edmund as the pre-eminent moral agent in the play not because he, like Cordelia, is eminently 'good', but because he is the only character in the play who acknowledges the universe as contingent, a powerful metaphysical insight which only he achieves.

This inner transformation is made outer in his attempt to save Cordelia's life. Whatever one thinks of Cordelia, it remains ambiguous by play's end whether she, through her initial transgression, manages to uphold the good or initiate the unfolding of evil. If the latter, it would hardly be fair to hold Cordelia *responsible* for the play's tragedy. But in order for the tragedy of *King Lear* to register, we must, at the very least, consider the possibility of her evil – the sort of possibility we become deaf to once we know how the play turns out.

The distinction between 'radical necessity' and 'radical contingency' is raised by Cavell. A consideration of these terms is more prominent in Kent Cartwright's use of Cavell. In particular, Cartwright appropriates and transfigures these terms to suit his discussion of tragedy:

> Stanley Cavell's essay 'The Avoidance of Love' explores the countervailing pulls of 'radical contingency' and 'radical necessity', qualities fundamental to Shakespearean tragedy. The 'radical contingency' of tragedy is its sense that each death is 'inflicted' and therefore need not have happened. Yet no one knows how to have prevented it; so a 'radical necessity' haunts tragedy, as well. That 'enveloping of contingency and necessity by one another … is why the death that ends a tragedy strikes one as inexplicable, necessary, but we do not know why; avoidable, but we do not know how; wrapped in meaning, but the meaning has come out, and so wrapped in mystery'. For Shakespearean tragedy, I associate 'engagement' with the audience's experience of 'radical necessity' and 'detachment' with its experience of 'radical contingency'.[1]

Cartwright's definition of 'engagement' is 'the spectator's surrender of self-awareness'.[2] To be 'engaged' with a play is to watch a play in the present, forgoing such awareness. 'Detachment', on the other hand, 'involves 'conception': insights and ideas',[3] and occurs, for the most part, post-performance. Though Cartwright notes that '[e]ngagement and detachment dance together',[4] thus 'stimulat[ing] an expansive sense of choice',[5] he firmly has engagement later validated by 'distance [detachment], the very ground of truth'.[6] Yet this refiguration and appropriation of Cavell's terms do a disservice to Cavell's reading of the play. Because Cartwright defines 'engagement' as an audience's 'surrender of self-awareness', what he is taking 'engagement' to mean is what Cavell means when he says 'presentness'. If tragedy, for Cavell, is rooted in a feeling of 'continuous presentness', moreover, then what Cavell means is that we are aware of necessity in the moment, which Cartwright alludes to; but we are also, simultaneously, contemporaneously, aware of contingency. To say Cavell's idea of 'radical contingency' is only pertinent when considering a play after the fact is to say that in watching a play, we are (simply) waiting for necessity to play out. What constitutes the necessary, however, can only be known or reflected upon after the fact. It would be far more profitable to reverse this distinction, to say that 'engagement' is associated with a 'radical contingency' and that post-facto 'distance', or 'spectatorial criticism',[7] is rooted in a push to establish necessity. Cartwright touches on this when he says that 'particularly for the modern spectator, necessity may only emerge as necessity after the fact'.[8] Here, Cartwright *is* equating necessity with detachment, though earlier, he has equated the perception of necessity via audience response with something closer to engagement. This inconsistency is not a mere trifle; the ramifications of where and when and how an understanding of contingency happens are worth sorting out. Cartwright, for example, never offers a well-wrought opinion on whether or not tragedy can exist on the page. In seeking to establish the primacy of his 'spectatorial' criticism, he takes for granted that the tragic effect is wholly, or perhaps fully, felt in performance; its articulation, however, comes only in hindsight via criticism, with the aid, no doubt, of the written text. Cartwright's 'dance' between performance and criticism is indeed a form of oscillation, but one occurring between 'engaged' performance and 'detached' (re)-reading of the text. The sort of oscillation worth attending to, however, is between competing versions of the present, the actual and the possible, accessible not to reading per se, but to reading for the first time.

In the previous chapter, we touched upon how Bradley manages to read *Hamlet* this way. In terms of charting responses, he notes that in performance, we judge a play's 'intelligibility' in a different way. Arguably, Bradley – in reminding us that in performance, Hamlet's delay may be the only action warranted – means that what we are tuned into when we see him delay is the necessity of the delay. In such a case, the 'radical contingency' of the act is only perceived after the play is over. Perhaps Cartwright is correct after all. In the present moment, are we more in tune with necessity or contingency? Cavell shows how in the moment we are aware of both. My reading of *Hamlet* highlighted both necessity and contingency as competing interpretations. Post-facto criticism, however, attempts to tip the scales of interpretation definitively in favour of necessity. Though Cartwright desires that post-facto criticism reclaim contingency, he does not believe contingency can be captured in the present. If a character's intelligibility is not necessarily compromised by the seemingly contingent in the present, however, what good is it to make it, somehow, necessary – hence explainable by appeal to the past? Do we need a *cause* for the contingent? If we get that, then we are removed from the realm of contingency and the mystery of tragedy is lost.

Articulating the differences between 'contingency' and 'necessity' on the one hand, and 'performance' and 'criticism' on the other, seems to marry an appreciation of the contingent to performance, and that of necessity to criticism. In order to make the case, then, that an appreciation of the contingent is perfectly accessible to criticism (and not just to performance in the present), let us now consider the ontological properties of the word, both on the page and on the stage. Cavell provides some guidance on the ontological properties of theatre as opposed to life:

> [W]hat is the difference between tragedy in a theater and tragedy in actuality? In both, people in pain are in our presence. But in actuality acknowledgement is incomplete; in actuality there is no acknowledgment, unless we put ourselves in their presence, reveal ourselves to them. We may find that the point of tragedy in a theater is exactly relief from this necessity, a respite within which to prepare for this necessity, to clean out the pity and terror which stand in the way of acknowledgment outside.[9]

The very conventions of theatre allow us to do nothing when we see Othello throttling Desdemona. We may say something like, 'we know he (the actor playing Othello) is not really strangling (the actress playing) Desdemona'. Nonetheless, the ethical imperative to do something as some horror is being played out before us is what the particular conventions of theatre take away. Because such an act is occurring immediately in our presence, it makes sense to imagine someone screaming out for Othello not to do the deed. The aesthetic value of watching some horror happen right before our eyes and of *not* being called upon to act, however, indeed being denied the opportunity to act, is part of (stage) tragedy's horror and pleasure.

Elsewhere, commenting on the conventional properties of cinema, Cavell notes that the screen allows us to be 'mechanically absent'[10] from proceedings. Frames of film pass before our eyes in the past tense. A world on film is a world in the past, already in the can. It makes no sense for someone viewing a screen adaptation of *Othello* to shout out in a cinema. Even if such a thing has occurred (doubtless it has), what has happened is that a particular individual has managed to watch cinema *like theatre*. This is not a mass, collective phenomenon. The lone spectator shouting out at the playhouse, however, is committing a transgression everyone in the theatre can sympathise with. In a theatre, the actors are in our presence; though we are tempted with the *possibility* of participation, the conventions of theatre deny us any possible participation. A screen actor, on the other hand, though interrupting our present, is mechanically absent. We watch a world dead to us. It makes no sense to imagine any possible participation, and lacking this key participatory element, we have reason to believe that cinema cannot elicit or draw out the tragic effect. But what about the page? Does it make sense to cry out, in the privacy of a reading room, for Othello not to do the deed?

Cartwright's title, *Shakespearean Tragedy and Its Double*, is a call out to Antonin Artaud and his key text on the ontology of theatre, *The Theatre and Its Double*. In his preface, Cartwright says he hopes his title 'might suggest both a Bradleyan attention to the details of the tragic world and an Artaudian concern for the effect of performance upon an audience'.[11] From this Cartwright establishes his peculiar 'double', that is, a 'double' viewing of the plays, at once 'engaged' and also 'detached', from which we are to gauge 'the rhythms of audience response'. Such is the methodology of what Cartwright calls a 'spectatorial criticism', allowing us to chart out as accurately as we can the

tragic effect. In short, Bradley offers engagement, attention to detail, while Artaud offers a concept of distance.
Yet this is a strange refiguration of Artaud as well, particularly when Cartwright says that Artaud 'wished to use
the theater's resources to obliterate the distinction between
life and drama'.[12] Yet, immediately following this sentence,
Cartwright entrenches his claim that '[d]istance determines
spectatorial experience – and ultimately tragic meaning'.[13]
Artaud, who does not comment specifically on tragedy in
his book, never promotes distance as any sort of ideal to
be achieved in the theatre. In wanting to obliterate the distinction between life and drama, he seeks greater intimacy
and incorporation of theatre into daily life. Moreover, he
goes so far as to equate theatre with 'contagious delirium'[14]
and 'alchemy',[15] stressing not the importance of speech,
but the importance of those gestures and objects which
come before speech as a means to exploit theatre's true
ontic potential. On the strengths of the Balinese (Oriental)
theatre as opposed to our Western (Occidental) theatre,
Artaud says

> [t]he Balinese theater has revealed to us a physical and
> non-verbal idea of the theater, in which the theater is con-
> tained within the limits of everything that can happen on
> a stage, independently of the written text, whereas the
> theater as we conceive it in the Occident has declared its
> alliance with the text and finds itself limited by it. For
> the Occidental theater the Word is everything, and there
> is no possibility of expression without it; the theater is a
> branch of literature, a kind of sonorous species of lan-
> guage, and even if we admit a difference between the text
> spoken on the stage and the text read by the eyes, if we
> restrict theater to what happens between cues, we have
> still not managed to separate it from the idea of a per-
> formed text.[16]

The likening of theatre to 'contagion' is a metaphorical ploy by Artaud to describe the coming into being on stage of something we might otherwise take to be magical: the daemonic quest to bring forth possibilities, not a re-presentation of something that already exists, but the presentation (on stage) of that which has yet to come into being. Accessing this realm of 'shadows', theatre's ostensible double, can only occur where language breaks off. The theatre, in order to inflict its brand of contagion upon its spectators, must unlock, unearth and present to the senses the sum total of energies lying latent behind our normal, day-to-day conception of the world. The 'double' is not the 'real' any more than theatre is fake. The theatre, like the plague, 'releases conflicts, disengages powers, liberates possibilities, and if these possibilities and these powers are dark, it is the fault not of the plague nor of the theater, but of life'.[17]

Hence Artaud's insistence on the veritable danger and cruelty of the theatre. In likening theatre to alchemy, Artaud further notes the ferocity which accompanies alchemy, the examination of everyday objects to the point where the meaning ascribed to them – whether spiritual, moral, practical – leaves us, ultimately, not with gold, but with a type of 'spiritualized gold'[18] through which darker forces are made manifest. Theatre, like poetry, is anarchical 'to the degree that it brings into play all the relationships of object to object and form to signification ... [and] to the degree that its occurrence is the consequence of a disorder that draws us closer to chaos'.[19] Clearly Artaud is taking us to the realm of Dionysus, and, furthermore, he says that our ability to inhabit such a realm could only be curtailed by language.

> All true feeling is in reality untranslatable. To express it is to betray it. But to translate it is to dissimulate it. True

> expression hides what it makes manifest. It sets the mind in
> opposition to the real void of nature by creating in reaction
> a kind of fullness in thought. Or, in other terms, in reaction
> to the manifestation-illusion of nature it creates a void in
> thought. All powerful feeling produces in us the idea of the
> void. And the lucid language which obstructs the appear-
> ance of this void also obstructs the appearance of poetry
> in thought. That is why an image, an allegory, a figure that
> masks what it would reveal have more significance for the
> spirit than the lucidities of speech and its analytics.[20]

Language lulls us into the belief that once something is
expressed lucidly, all there is (to be expressed) has been
expressed. Whatever the void, it is, ultimately, nothing, so
how could language capture the void? It could only mask it,
however lucidly spoken.

How, then, could even the lucid presentation or articulation of lost possibilities hope to do any better? Artaud,
in making his case for non-verbal theatre, in calling for
Occidental theatre as we know it to be 'destroyed with
diligence and malice on every level',[21] is not making any
particular plea for tragedy. Nietzsche, moreover, who
reminds us that tragedy is born once we are able to recognise and even sanctify the destructive forces of Dionysus in our dramaturgy, does not say that tragedy lives
solely in Dionysian festival, but that it lives in the oscillation between Apollo and Dionysus, in the recognition that
each needs theother. He goes on to say that tragedy is born
out of the spirit of music because music is non-verbal.
Artaud likewise nominates the importance of music, along
with 'dance, plastic art, pantomime, mimicry, gesticulation, intonation, architecture, lighting, and scenery'.[22] If
the form and harmony of music are Apollonian enough,
where does this leave us with regard to Shakespeare?
We know that however it is that he manages to elicit the

tragic, the 'shadows', it is *because* of his words. Do his words supplement the pantomime, mimicry and gesticulation of Elizabethan theatre or do these things supplement Shakespeare?

First we must note that Shakespearean verse carries musical properties and the musical property of verse draws us in, increases intimacy with the particular narrative unfolding. To return to the question of whether we feel compelled to shout out at Othello in the privacy of a reading room, the suggestion here is that imagining counterfactuals as we read is the way *we do* shout out in private. Counterfactual possibilities are silenced not by the presence of the text per se, but first, by the narrative as it unfolds, and second, by the words or acts of criticism that, in their very zeal to explain the void or sense of reader helplessness, do more to mask the void in unprofitable ways. Fleshing out counterfactual alternatives is to bypass critical analysis temporarily and attach the spirit of music to Shakespearean verse. Attending to lost possibilities goes some way in addressing or acknowledging what is rendered non-verbal on stage. Hence counterfactual criticism is sympathetic to what Artaud believes theatre ought to be in the business of promoting: the non-verbal manifestation of feeling.

Posing counterfactual alternatives places the reader on the edge of discovery. Jeffrey Kahan, for example, engages in this bit of counterfactual speculation over Cordelia's death:

> Yes, Cordelia has to die, but, even within the bounds of his other tragedies, Shakespeare had a variety of more palatable options. Shakespeare might have staged it akin to Romeo and Juliet's demise. Lear comes on carrying his daughter, dies of a broken heart, Cordelia then revives, sees her father and dies. Or, he might have done it along the lines of Othello: Lear carries her in, she

revives, forgives her father for starting all this mess, then dies, prompting the king to kill himself. The difference between these plays and Lear is one of expectation. Since in *Romeo and Juliet* the plot-turn depends upon playing dead and we know it's a tragedy and we're in the fifth act and she's lying there and Romeo has poison, we expect it to all go wrong. Having plotted Desdemona's death, Othello's and our own surprise is merely that she awakens long enough to forgive him. With respect to the fact of her death, it is both expected and, occurring as it does in the fifth act, necessary to a neat close. But the death of Cordelia is not the sacrifice of an innocent victim, nor is it presented with poetic justification. Indeed, given that in Act 4, scene 6 Lear awoke thinking he was dead, might we not here also expect in Act 5, scene 3 for Cordelia to do the same?[23]

Kahan is asking not so much whether Cordelia's death is necessary as whether the manner of her death is necessary. The critical imperative is to establish necessity, or the necessary conditions around which we can judge a play, or an ending, to be adequate or palatable. The curious reach for criteria to account for necessity beyond the play itself (to *Romeo and Juliet* and *Othello*) mirrors the sorts of New Historicist reaches for evidence, of some sort, to ground our understanding. Yet in order to chart out responses, we must try to read *Lear* for the first time, as Frye manages to do here:

When you start to read or listen to *King Lear*, try to pretend that you've never heard the story before, and forget that you know how bad Goneril and Regan and Edmund are going to be. That way, you'll see more clearly how Shakespeare is building up our sympathies in the opposite direction.[24]

We discussed how Shakespeare toys with his own audiences' assumptions (of the *Leir* tale) and how, according to Greenblatt, his novel presentation of the opening scenes makes Lear's motives 'more strange and arbitrary'. Frye's comments complement Greenblatt's nicely because both remind us that our present-day reception of the text is likely to be skewed by the assumptions we bring to the text. Where Greenblatt wants to establish a reason or justification for us to begin, with the benefit of historical hindsight, to question or doubt Lear's motives, Frye's reminder does more to counteract this initial certainty. Greenblatt wants to tie our doubt to a sort of historicist's necessity, while Frye, in championing a type of certainty or 'coolness' to the play's first scenes, leaves open the possibility of more counterfactual discussion because he reminds us how vulnerable we are to coming contingencies.

> In the first two acts, all Lear's collisions with his daughters steadily diminish his dignity and leave them with the dramatic honours. They never lose their cool: they are certainly harsh and unattractive women, but they have a kind of brusque common sense that bears him down every time.[25]

It is difficult to tell whether Frye is criticising in hindsight when he says that Regan and Goneril are 'harsh and unattractive', because there is no immediate correlation between 'brusque common sense' and unattractiveness. What is entirely clear, however, is that Frye shows us how perfectly reasonable it is to ally ourselves with Regan and Goneril, that their responses to Lear's outbursts are, in a way, the only ones warranted. We may not be ready to condemn Cordelia, but her responses leave us suspicious, more so than those of her sisters.

The banality of the coming love test (that it could be read as a rather banal staging of events) is registered in Kent's opening exchange with Gloucester:

> KENT. I thought the king had more affected the Duke of Albany than Cornwall.
> GLOUCESTER. It did always seem so to us; but now, in the division of the kingdom, it appears not which of the dukes he values most: for equalities are so weighted, that the curiosity in neither can make choice of either's moiety.   (1.1.1–6)

The coming standoff has been accepted by those at court as a playing out of mere formality. Between Albany and Cornwall there is no essential difference; the coming division of the kingdom should proceed rather uneventfully. Furthermore, Act 1, scene 1 actually ends happily. Cordelia is taken by France, dowerless, saving us a fair amount of moral anguish. Even if we are, at this point, suspicious of either Lear or his other two daughters (or both), we also take comfort knowing that good has been banished hence and evil is left to contend with evil – a situation more comic than tragic. However dramatic we may believe the opening scenes to be, our recollection of them as dramatic occurs largely in hindsight. Frye even notes a mood of semi-charged banality governing the first two acts entirely.

Frye's reading, which downplays the opening drama, seems to *contradict* Greenblatt's, which explicitly elevates it. That Greenblatt is describing a likely Elizabethan response, and Frye, perhaps, a more contemporary response, does not necessarily restrict each sort of response to a particular historical timeframe. Perhaps Elizabethan audiences were afforded as much opportunity for doubt as for calm, just as we are today. It is easy enough to take a position of strength with regard to our knowledge of the play, once the play is over, thereby to assume we had reason all along to doubt Lear's motives. However, what counterfactual speculation advances is not the validity of such critical postures of strength but the possibility of reader weakness, of reader unknowingness. Do we know that Cordelia is good and her sisters evil at the end of Act 1? How about at the end of Act 2? When, indeed, do we know? Even at the end, after all the waste and loss of human life, we are left feeling that were it to occur again, Cordelia should simply take her third of the kingdom and be silent. In hindsight, perhaps Hamlet ought to have done the deed. In hindsight, perhaps Cordelia ought not to have done hers. Neither of these normative claims could be made in the present. What we want, what tragedy reminds us we cannot have, is the knowledge necessary to make these sorts of normative statements on the fly. That we are barred from such knowledge is tragic.

Criticism which touches on our ability or need to forgo knowledge comes closer to capturing the essence of tragedy, and not because such criticism reminds us that simply by forgoing knowledge we can avert disaster. Rather, if tragedy is a problem of knowledge, it is a problem of knowledge arriving too late, not to our benefit, and there is nothing we can do in the present to summon it. To deprive ourselves of the knowledge gained with the benefit of hindsight is to reclaim this sort of understanding *for ourselves*. Kahan's later embrace of contingency is far more apposite to his discussion of tragedy. Commenting specifically on Edmund, he notes:

> Edmund worships Nature, which changes season-by-season and day-by-day. To be at one with Nature, Edmund has to be equally polymorphic: bold, admirable and resolute as well as furtive, worthless and perfidious. Not surprisingly, Edmund's triumphs are as fleeting as his personae. Moreover, given that Edmund wins the war and loses his

life, we may ponder whether his gains are any less illusory
than Lear's. In this regard, the play is neither joyous nor
gloomy. One character may express encouraging thoughts
at one moment, discouraging thoughts in another, one may
say something that seems lucid or mad, but each statement
is no more authoritative or less transient than another. In
King Lear, people take pleasure where they can and hope
that their gains are real and lasting, but hope is not the
same as certainty.[26]

Commentary like this seems the last word on *King Lear*, a
surrender of our critical faculties and an embrace of contingency. This seems to entail further that the 'lesson' of tragedy
is some banal acceptance of the unknown.

The idea that Edmund worships nature is taken from his
injunction to it ('Thou, nature, art my goddess. To thy law /
My services are bound' (1.2.1–2) and Kahan's reading implies
that Edmund, like nature, operates under, or embraces, a certain amount of unpredictability in the cosmos, as though set
patterns of human relationships (in distinguishing between
legitimate and bastard children) are themselves the sources
of injustice; indeed, he invokes a certain rough justice when
he appeals 'gods, stand up for bastards!' (1.2.22). The unpredictability of the unfolding of seasons or days is perhaps
cause for anxiety. It is also true, however, that the seasons
and days – that is, what Kahan here associates with nature –
can be thought of as entirely *predictable*, that their period-
icity mirrors (indeed, is directly tied to) that of the movement of the planets and stars in their orbits. This brings us
to Gloucester's panicked interpretation after witnessing the
initial division of Lear's household and reading of Edgar's
forged letter:

These late eclipses in the sun and moon portend no good
to us. Though the wisdom of nature can reason it thus

and thus, yet nature finds itself scourged by the sequent effects. Love cools, friendship falls off, brothers divide; in cities, mutinies; in countries, discord; in palaces, treason; and the bond cracked 'twixt son and father ... We have seen the best of our time. Machinations, hollowness, treachery, and all ruinous disorders follow us disquietly to our graves.　　　　　　　　　　　　　　(1.2.95–105)

If there is indeed wisdom in the movement of the sun and the moon, and if this wisdom portends future strife, what Gloucester is doing here is at once asserting the authority of nature ('the wisdom of nature can reason it thus and thus') while denying its very wisdom ('yet nature finds itself scourged by the sequent effects'). In the end, he is saying that the coming unpredictability is entirely predictable, as a means, no doubt, of reassuring himself against the fact that he knows not *what* will come. He can only assume the worst. It is this sort of exclusive reasoning that Edmund chides his father for. Edmund himself knows not what will come. He desires a certain amount of 'discord', appeals directly to nature for it, is himself actively committing treason. But to assert that his father's worst fears, or even his own success, are a matter of necessity is not a step he is willing to take:

This is the excellent foppery of the world: that when we are sick in fortune – often the surfeit of our own behavior – we make guilty of our disasters [or our successes for that matter] the sun, the moon, and stars, as if we were villains [or heroes] on necessity.　　　　　　(1.2.108–11)

Kahan says Edmund is 'bold'. Indeed, his boldness is in his ability not to overcome the contingent, but to embrace it, to accept his own weakness rather than hastily asserting his strength.

CURAN. Have you heard of no likely wars toward twixt
   the Dukes of Cornwall and Albany?
EDMOND. Not a word.
CURAN. You may do then in time. Fare you well, sir.
EDMOND. The Duke be here tonight! The better, best.
This weaves itself perforce into my business.   (2.1.6–15)

Edmund's implausible string of luck has been brought to critical attention before. Coleridge notes that Edmund operates
within a 'concurrence of circumstance and accident', though
he notes that even without the benefit of accident and circumstance, 'pride will necessarily be the sin that most easily
besets him'.[27] Yet pride does not completely beset him. In the
final act, Edmund offers a complete reversal of his previous
actions when he says 'Some good I mean to do, / Despite of
my own nature' (5.3.217–18). Nothing he said previously
in the time of the play necessitates his coming change of
heart. Furthermore, at this point, he seems to be castigat-
ing everything he has done previously *as* evil. Initially, however, Edmund *had* meant to do some good. He appealed, for
instance, to nature and the gods (Iago appeals to 'hell' itself
(2.3.324)) to stand up for bastards. His previous acts become
evil in the most meaningful sense only when he himself con-
demns them as such and for no apparent or easily explicable
reason. Edmund transforms in the manner of a convert. And
no matter how we may try to trace the steps to conversion,
conversion itself is a radically contingent act, a rupture of
necessity beyond the realm of explanation. There is no *reason*
true conversion should happen at all. We may tell ourselves
it is more *likely* at the tail end of intense moral and spiritual suffering, making it believable, necessary. But what *King
Lear* documents is not successful conversion, but ultimately,
arguably, failed conversion – whether Lear's, Gloucester's
or Edgar's; only Edmund's is successful. We may say it is
fatuous, that he has not undergone the requisite spiritual

austerity to make such conversion believable, hence his conversion occurs as a matter of (conventional) necessity. But this is to say that we are not given the materials with which to trace out his conversion. Edmund's sudden desire to do good, like Cordelia's death, is a wholly and radically contingent act. Nothing can prepare us for either. Edmund seems motivated by nothing other than a desire to act 'despite of [his] own nature', to thwart necessity.

The type of 'spectatorial criticism' Cartwright espouses is the sort that takes us away from the play, loading up experience with the type of speculation that distances us from it. Abstract theories meant to gauge audience response do little to explain why we felt the play tragic upon viewing it on stage or reading it on the page for the first time. Even Brecht, who says that Shakespeare's plays are full of 'alienation effects',[28] believes we must *remain* alienated from the play in order to brood over its (social) implications post-performance. Alienation occurs not at a distance in time, but in the present. As Artaud argues, theatre immerses our consciousness in the becoming of the present. In wanting to acknowledge such becoming through a consideration of speech, we need only consider the possibilities latent and lost in speech, understanding that speech does, indeed, 'mask', rather than (re)present.

One can read *King Lear* as an exploration of necessity gone wrong and not because the necessary is a priori evil. Indeed, if the comedies teach us anything, it is that the necessary and the good often go hand in hand. In tragedy, it is not the hubris of those on the bottom that disrupts the moral order. Rather, and more pressingly, tragedy documents the inability of those who benefit from the moral order to represent, or see clearly, how contingent the good of the universe truly is, thereby taking the good for granted. *King Lear* does not thematise the burden of the past or our misjudgements of the past. More specifically, the play emphasises that to exist in the present means being open to the possibility of either good or evil at every turn. This is not to say that either good or evil is *necessary* at every turn; merely that in being open to possibilities, to conversion, we mean to do some good, to 'see better', despite our natures. Gloucester and Lear did not mean to do good. They reneged on the possibility of good, believing the love of their children was a matter of necessity. When that necessity was lost, or compromised, they had not the means or ability to cope with the possibility that the love even of their 'loyal' children was also a matter of contingency. They suffered from what Bradley calls 'want of imagination',[29] a deficiency in the liminal space required to consider moral possibilities. Edmund, by play's end, is (still) armed with the *possibility* of doing good. He refuses to be cornered by necessity, and, in a way, invites us to do the same. He takes up his chance, and though unsuccessful, he, at least, can still mean to do some good.

Yet the simple prescription that Lear and Gloucester, and even Edgar, extend their imaginative faculties to accommodate more possibilities cannot provide us with a suitable *moral*. For, in effect, this is what Cordelia does. She extends her imaginative faculties, seeing her father fully, in all his vulnerability, in the hope ultimately that he will see her. If we are to judge these characters by their lack of expansiveness, there is no easy way to know, in the present, when to expand our minds and thereby expose ourselves to others, or when to retract, or make ourselves smaller to the world, to accept its conventions without controversy.

The love test was staged not for Cordelia, but for Lear. Lear, and not Cordelia, failed the test because she was trying to create the space for him to consider the possible, to have him believe that her love was not a matter of mere necessity. Because we can only know Lear fails the test in hindsight, however, it makes no sense for us as critics to affirm that we knew all along that Cordelia's intentions were good.

Such thinking removes us from the presentness of the play, is itself a plea for necessity which leaves us blind to the possibility of Cordelia's evil, or, less dramatically, her wrongdoing (a possibility we are more in tune with when reading *Lear* for the first time), what Coleridge calls her 'sullenness',[30] what Frye implies is a lack of common sense. We have every right to castigate Cordelia precisely as Lear does. Whether Shakespeare intended us to do so or not is not the issue. Part of the tragedy of *King Lear* involves repenting our own hasty condemnation of Cordelia, usually by imagining we would never have condemned her in the first place. We forget also, in hindsight, Edmund's good. His conversion has us falling over ourselves trying to come to terms with its inexplicability, precisely to hide from the fact that in the beginning, Edmund's desire for justice is worth a friendly ear. If Cordelia seeks to remove Lear's dependence on the past, wishes him to see in the present, then so too does Shakespeare's ambiguous presentation of events (our arrival at court *in medias res*) invite consideration by his readers of the possible, of both Edmund's good and Cordelia's evil.

Lastly, in the case of *Lear*, it is difficult to know what we are screaming out for anyone to do. Even when the play ends and some semblance of moral order takes shape, we are left unsure as to what anyone could have done to avoid the outcome we are given. To move forward on a commitment to do good, despite whatever surrounding conventions demand, can be perilous indeed. What is left when necessity, or utility, provide us a world in which moral choice is negated by virtue of performing our necessary duties out of politeness? (Cordelia, even if virtuous, is *rude*.) Do we protect the shallow views of our loved ones, or try to create the space for conversion to happen, even at considerable risk? Is Cordelia heroic, or foolish? Counterfactual thinking allows us to entertain her terrible *foolishness*, to formulate an 'anti-Cordelia' reading neither too hasty in condemning her nor too bombastically sanctimonious. From without, the default stance of *Lear* criticism, Cordelia's death is heroic, wholly necessary. From within, her death is wholly foolish, entirely contingent. If Cordelia were alive today, carrying out her stunts right before our eyes, we could do nothing *but* roll our eyes. To those who knew Cordelia, who avoid the rush to sanctify her and instead embrace the rush of the present, her life and example are a tragic waste indeed.

CHAPTER 4

STAGING PASSIVITY: COUNTERFACTUAL THINKING AND *MACBETH*

To consider counterfactual possibilities is to consider, and to want to rescue, a character's freedom. It reflects a critical desire to break from limitations, or limitations of convention. In *Macbeth*, we are presented with a prophecy that seems to limit the possible ways the play could end. In *Hamlet* we are given not prophecy, but testimony, which does not restrict Hamlet's freedom in the same way. It makes sense for both Hamlet and us as readers to question the veracity of the Ghost's story. We can conceive of the possibility of the Ghost as a 'Goblin damned' (1.4.21), however much we may want its testimony to be true. In *Macbeth*, on the other hand, to ask something like 'What if the prophecies aren't true?' would be to ask, 'If not, why would Shakespeare give them to us?' And there is no answer other than to reiterate that because he does, it is by matter of conventional necessity that they come true. Hence no serious critical effort can question the veracity of the sisters' prophecy in the way Greg called 'Hamlet's hallucination' into question. The Ghost's appearance in *Hamlet* does not dictate as explicitly in what manner Hamlet *ought* to unfold. The sisters' prophecy, on the other hand, does have immediate bearing on how *Macbeth*, and not Macbeth, should end. At some point, Macbeth must serve, or have served, as king. This suggests that Macbeth is far more beholden to outer necessity rather than inner contingency, which further shrinks his sphere of individuality and hence his freedom. So how indeed to (re)capture Macbeth's freedom? If it is imperative for us, as readers, to remember that Macbeth *is* free, we must consider what sort of critical price we are willing to pay for his freedom.

One way would be to delay, as long as possible, a definitive reading of the precise arrival of Macbeth's ambition. Where Hamlet is burdened by the (im)possibility of correct action, Macbeth is burdened by the (im)possibility of correct thought. Hamlet desires thought as an end to all thinking, as though once armed with correct thought, correct action can only follow. Macbeth operates at an opposite metaphysical pole. He desires correct action as an end to all action, as though once the correct action is carried out, he will no longer be burdened by his desires.

> If chance will have me king, why, chance may crown me
> Without my stir.   (1.3.142–3)

The appeal to chance here suggests that Macbeth *does not* want to act at all. Indeed, one reads in these lines the possibility of a Macbeth who chooses not to murder Duncan, who rests on his laurels and waits for the sisters' prophecy to unfold.

Clearly Macbeth is stirred by the sisters' prophecy in a way Banquo is not:

> MACBETH (to the WITCHES). Speak, if you can. What are you?
> FIRST WITCH. All hail, Macbeth! Hail to thee, Thane of Glamis.
> SECOND WITCH. All hail, Macbeth! Hail to thee, Thane of Cawdor.

THIRD WITCH. All hail, Macbeth, that shalt be King
  hereafter!
BANQUO. Good sir, why do you start and seem to fear
Things that do sound so fair?

The obvious reading here, necessarily formulated in hindsight, is that Macbeth has been outed by the sisters, that they
have given voice to a desire Macbeth holds secretly in his heart.
The reason he is somewhat flummoxed is that he fears he will
be (has been) found out; hence we are to conclude that he has
had designs of murdering Duncan all along. That Macbeth
feels ashamed of desiring the crown is a plausible interpretation. Yet it is equally plausible that Macbeth feels ashamed of
desiring. What he is startled by is not that his ambitions have
become known to others but that suddenly, they are known
to *him*, made known, given voice and a preliminary expression. What Macbeth desires primarily is something akin to
metaphysical rest, conceived by Hamlet as an end to all thinking, by Macbeth as an end to all action, so no longer need-
ing to heed, or subordinate oneself to, the perpetual call to
act. Macbeth feels ashamed not of desiring the crown, but of
being restless, unsatisfied with his lot. The immediate temptation is not (necessarily) to murder Duncan. That only becomes
tempting when this particular path is *suggested to him* by
circumstances and contingencies outside of his control. The
question is whether it is wrong or immoral or tragic to want
(merely) or demand this sort of metaphysical rest in the first
place, as an end in itself. To desire such rest a priori is to make
oneself vulnerable or susceptible to outside influence, to suggestion, particularly because no one can ever know, from the
outset, what exactly it will take to curb our desires.

Macbeth, like Edmund, is open to conversion. Unlike
Edmund, however, he does not have moral imagination
enough to understand what his own nature is, which is
partly why Macbeth makes himself beholden to the stars,

something Edmund refuses to do. Does Macbeth have a choice? What a prophecy entails – in a play, for instance – is that he does not. Where Shakespeare allies us with Edmund's knowledge that to take another's word as necessary is indeed to make a foppery of the world in *King Lear*, he situates us within an otherworldly or supernatural necessity through the sisters' prophecies in *Macbeth*. In a way, it seems we are *supposed to* make a foppery of the world. We cannot seek out verification of the prophecies in the way we do in *Hamlet*. We demand verification in *Macbeth* in a different way, so not to receive it would make the play unintelligible.

> MACBETH. This supernatural soliciting
> Cannot be ill, cannot be good. If ill,
> Why hath it given me earnest of success
> Commencing in a truth? I am Thane of Cawdor.
> If good, why do I yield to that suggestion
> Whose horrid image doth unfix my hair
> And make my seated heart knock at my ribs
> Against the use of nature? Present fears
> Are less than horrible imaginings.
> My thought, whose murder yet is but fantastical,
> Shakes so my single state of man that function
> Is smothered in surmise, and nothing is
> But what is not.   (1.3.129–41)

The 'horrible imaginings' suggests that whatever Macbeth fears, whatever possibilities are brewing in his mind, they are mediated by less than noble desires, again suggesting that Macbeth's thoughts here are black, in no way innocent.

Even here, after Ross and Angus have named him Thane of Cawdor, Macbeth is still unsure as to how to receive the sisters' prophecy, as something either 'good' or 'ill'. The prophecy is more or less taken in jest by Banquo. For Macbeth, on the other hand, it is not the case that the sisters have 'outed' him, because he is still uncertain as to what has been outed. The anxiety he feels is of not knowing, of being forced to consider now not the single state of his existence in this world, but the number of possibilities that the sisters' prophecy might entail. This is where Macbeth's freedom resides, a freedom he detests. His existence is suddenly 'smothered in surmise' and what 'is' has been made subordinate to what might be, what at present 'is not'.

The editors of the *Norton Shakespeare* paraphrase line 138 of Act 1, scene 3 ('My thought, whose murder yet is but fantastical') as follows: 'In which murder is so far only a fantasy'. The question then is, the murder of whom, or what? We may be quick to reply, 'Duncan', but the less forced interpretation is that Macbeth is explicitly discussing, hence desiring, the murder of (his) thought, only 'fantastical' at present because his thought cannot grasp or get a hold over the infinitude of his desire, the limitless number of possibilities the sisters' prophecy entails. Macbeth wants to murder thought so that 'function' can (once again) follow. He desires the division of his self, amongst a plethora of possibilities not yet given voice, to be made whole again – preferably, of course, by a single voice, recommending a single course of action. One could here interpret that Macbeth does indeed desire thought in order to murder action. What he really desires, however, is the correct action, or function, that will murder thought and hence, subsequent calls to action. Macbeth, unlike Hamlet, intuits that thought will not save him – only action will, and only if successful in murdering thought.

It is not the means to an end that is prophesied; *it is the ends only*. Strangely, the prophecy does not *limit* Macbeth's action. The prophecy alone unleashes a torrent of metaphysical possibilities. Furthermore, the note that appears in the middle of line 139 ('Shakes so my single state of man[1]') reads: 'My undivided self. Macbeth feels that his wholeness is coming apart under the pressure of his criminal thought.' Macbeth is coming apart under the pressure of thought, though whether it is truly criminal at this point cannot be known definitively.

Where his thoughts do turn criminal, definitively, is near the end of Act 1, scene 4, when he voices his desire to murder not Duncan, but his newly named heir, Malcolm, now Prince of Cumberland:

> MACBETH (aside). The Prince of Cumberland – that is a
>   step
> On which I must fall down or else o'erleap,
> For in my way it lies. Stars, hide your fires,
> Let not light see my black and deep desires;
> The eye wink at the hand; yet let that be
> Which the eye fears, when it is done, to see.   (1.4.48–53)

Obviously what Macbeth wants to hide is his desire, now taking more concrete shape through his contemplation of action. These desires seem to emanate outwards from within, so that outward show must hide 'black and deep desires'. To read these lines as bringing out something inner reverses the gradient of projection, however. What has taken place is the opposite: outer contingency has given shape to inner desire.

If we grant that Macbeth is unsure of how to act, because still unsure of how to think, we must try to find the sorts of outer contingencies that bring about something we might call conviction (at this point) in him. The line immediately preceding his earlier aside is by Duncan. He addresses Macbeth as 'My worthy Cawdor' (1.4.47), that is, by title, a naming which grounds Macbeth, and less makes him aware of his position in a regency than aware of the possibility, even the actuality, of his own advancement.[1]

This is not to imply that Macbeth is actually doomed once he has been addressed as Cawdor, which would be merely to defer the moment his fate is sealed, rather than reclaim his freedom.[2] Where counterfactual thinking is useful is in considering whether a world could exist where other options are available to Macbeth, where he is tempted to commit other deeds (rather than murder) to achieve the ends the sisters have prophesied for him. What if Macbeth had chosen not to act? We have already touched on the possibility of Macbeth essentially doing nothing, waiting for chance to take hold. It is not too difficult to imagine how such a possibility could play out. Macbeth could simply bide his time. A whole host of external events could happen to bring him to the crown. Duncan could simply fall ill and die, and then, somehow, both of his sons. One could argue here that it is simply not in Macbeth's nature to rest on his laurels, that he is all too willing to act, so that to suppose him capable of biding his time is to misread his character and the very nature of the play he dominates.

But this is to commit to saying that Macbeth is playing out a 'self-fulfilling prophecy', so that because he has been granted knowledge of his future, he takes pains to realise it. This sort of reading once again dooms Macbeth and necessitates that he act just as he does. If it is in the realm of possibility that he does nothing, and if such a possibility, in fact, *crosses his mind*, then why does he choose, instead, to act? We could appeal to all sorts of coming outer contingencies. Even if the resolve he gains in being addressed as Cawdor dissolves, other contingencies present themselves to reaffirm that resolve. Here we begin thinking of Lady Macbeth and her destructive influence on her husband. This is once again to delay the moment when we believe Macbeth is doomed, as though it is our critical lot to establish the precise moment his freedom is relinquished.

The most immediate reason Macbeth acts is because if he did not, *we would not have a very interesting play*. This seems obvious, trite. But when Bradley, extending Hegel's

discussion of dramatic poetry more forcefully to Shakespeare, says that

> the notion of tragedy as a conflict emphasizes the fact that
> action is the centre of the story, while the concentration of
> interest ... on the inward struggle emphasizes the fact that
> this action is essentially the expression of character[3]

he goes on to link the function of tragedy fundamentally to
character action, as though character is best expressed by
action. What does this say about the possibility of tragedy
coalescing around a character who refuses to act? Something
to the effect that whoever refuses to act has removed himself
from the realm of tragedy. Again, this seems obvious enough
at best, entirely unhelpful at worst. But another possible
implication, in restricting the function of tragedy to dramatic poetry, or narrative, or action, is that the stance of not
wanting to act, if indeed such a stance can be thought of as
tragic (if not dramatic), *must somehow be linked to action.*
What results is a fundamental incongruence between what
the character does and his motivations, in a sense delinking,
or at least loosening, the function of tragedy from character
action. Macbeth may indeed be tragic because he acts. To
induce then from his actions, however, that he wanted to act
all along, that he chose to act and so is responsible for his
fate, is far too limiting a proposition to sustain because, in
a way, Macbeth had no choice in the matter. So how does
this reading reclaim Macbeth's freedom? By separating him
from his actions in this way, it seems we are victimising him
instead. Macbeth cannot possibly be aware that he acts for
our dramatic pleasure.

Macbeth is responding to external contingencies rather
than playing out some internal necessity. These contingencies include supernatural voices (the sisters), mortal voices
(his wife) and signs (the daggers). Macbeth may be acting,

but he is acting *passively.* If he feels that desire is something to be avoided, he also feels that whatever action he must undertake must be rooted outside himself. Macbeth does not know whether the sisters' prophecy will lead to salvation or to damnation. What he does know is that ambition, naked and brutal ambition, is abhorrent and that the best way to avoid it is to avoid his own inner inclinations and instead be led by outer forces. How does one avoid tragedy? One might think: to curb infinite desire in *me* – which is what Macbeth does, or rather, *thinks.* In hindsight, we can say that Macbeth was a victim, that he could not see that he was, all along, being controlled by forces of desire and ambition ultimately housed in him, could not face or deal with his ostensible 'flaws'. But one could also read Macbeth as ultimately acting out a desire to confront, head on, hence to put away, his desire and ambition once and for all – the crown a symbol not of ambition rewarded, but of ambition put to rest. Hamlet wants to take arms against a sea of troubles by thinking, then acting. Macbeth wants to avoid any subsequent sea of troubles by acting, so to avoid thinking, or desiring, altogether. Both manifest a particular relationship to a type of knowledge from without: a verifiable sort in Hamlet's case leading, hopefully, to correct action; an absolute sort in Macbeth's leading, hopefully, to *no action.* This means that tragedy has more to do with our orientation to knowledge and how it affects character action, the sorts of possibilities *it* draws out, rather than the reverse. We are, indeed, more accustomed to assuming that action manifests some internal and stable character flaw. In the former scenario, character freedom is assured through the subsequent play of contingency. In the latter, necessity is established after the fact and the players – more violently, viciously – are victimised. Macbeth has not internalised the desire for self-aggrandisement and power we normally associate with moral monsters. His 'fate' is not testament to his ambition. Rather, his actions betray his desire to curb his own ambition.

Macbeth is not shameless, one interpretation of him being 'rapt withal' (1.3.55). Macbeth is 'rapt' with, startled by, the preliminary expression of a desire the origins of which he has reason to be suspicious of. Hence he has a desire to forgo revenge, realised dramatically through his gratuitous taking of revenge. Macbeth has little interest in inflating himself or his worth. ('I dare do all that may become a man; / Who dares do more is none' (1.7.46–7).) If indeed his ambition is dangerous, it is not because he is an egomaniac like Caligula or Tamburlaine. What Macbeth wants is to deflate himself, his worth, and the most expedient way to do this, he is made to believe, is to murder Duncan. Others can only interpret this as naked ambition. In a very real and significant way Macbeth's ambition is naked. He knows not how or with what to dress it. ('Why do you dress me / In borrowed robes?' (1.3.106–7)) But his ambition does not exist as an end in itself, insatiable to the point of continual expansion. Rather his ambition is insatiable to the point of unachievable contraction. He has a clear end in mind, and when this end proves unattainable, he no longer fears death but welcomes it. Which is worse: an articulated, known ambition that revels in itself as an end (revealed most cynically in the speech of the true Shakespearean Machiavels, Iago and Richard III), or unarticulated desire which does not revel in itself, desires an end, but cannot formulate in speech (in thought) the means of its achievement, as though knowing we are incapable of thinking our way past our desires anyway?

Shakespeare's great achievement with *Macbeth* is in the staging of passivity through dramatic action. Macbeth is a unique tragic hero. However much we may conceive of Hamlet as failing to act, we understand his soul and ambitions to be huge. In comparison, Macbeth's ambitions are small. If his desires are grandiose, it is their grandiosity he seeks to curb, all of which manifests itself through action which, at face value, suggests Macbeth is cravenly ambitious, that this flaw is at the root of his tragedy. With *Macbeth*, however, Shakespeare shows us, despite Hegelian or Bradleyan protestations to the contrary, *that action is no more indubitably linked to tragedy than is passivity.* Drama certainly requires action, but tragedy *not necessarily.*⁴ Moreover, tragedy is often construed, particularly in Cavellian studies, as having everything to do with desiring *too much,* hence the 'lesson' being, in a way, to desire less.⁵ But *Macbeth* shows us that even in desiring too little, or in wanting to desire too little, we are no more immune from tragedy. In a way, Macbeth *does* rest on his laurels. He *receives* the world, makes no demands upon it other than wanting to continue such rest. He is no less susceptible, however, to the play of contingency and the possibility of tragedy. Lastly, he is not unwilling to 'acknowledge finitude'. In fact, he all too stridently desires it. What he cannot acknowledge is *infinitude,* the infinitude of his desires.

CHAPTER 5

REVERSING TIME: COUNTERFACTUAL THINKING AND *THE WINTER'S TALE*

The idea that the march of history moves in a particular direction, developing in a linear fashion upward to irreversible progress, is one that dates from the nineteenth century. The nineteenth century, with its belief in the triumph of science and the spread of the catastrophic optimism of Marxist theories, was the period when those ideas superseded a concept of cyclical history characterized by regressions and leaps forward ... The birth of these views in the nineteenth century ... made it possible to establish the idea that time is a neutral quality that is measurable and is characterized by non-repetition. In the magic, primitive view, in contrast, time is apprehended as discontinuous (periods of disorder or festivity alternate with the everyday), uneven (some days are propitious, some unpropitious) and cyclical (by analogy with natural, organic rhythms).

François Laroque

François Laroque's comments about the passage of time as a nineteenth-century invention mirrors Steiner's critique of redemption and suggests that myths of reason are what set the mind in motion. Tragedy is reconceived as something no longer to be celebrated via ritual performance, but something the possible occurrence of which in human affairs must be prevented or avoided at all costs. The early modern conception of tragedy, moving inexorably away from ritual and country festival, is caught up in material fantasies of progress making its unfolding irreversible. A stagnant view of tragedy and its occurrence (revisiting it through ritual) is considered 'magic' and 'primitive' and is indicative of our surrender to fates outside of our control.

Paul A. Kottman, distinguishing between Attic and early modern tragedy, similarly registers the gravity of Shakespeare's achievement. On Attic tragedy first, Kottman notes:

> [T]ragic representation becomes central to civic discourse in moments at which the city seeks to question its own value or sustainability, as in fifth-century BCE Athens. Tragedies like *Oedipus* and *Antigone* ask us to consider how we can best ... transmit the conditions of living with one another ... Indeed, it may be that we come to measure the significance or value of our bodily lives together in terms of its worldly inheritability – the relative transmissibility of rights, entitlements, possessions, institutions, and prerogatives that we might wish to bestow on those we love.[1]

In Kottman's view, Attic tragedy thematises both the contingency and the necessity of the social customs we transmit to succeeding generations. Our entitlements, possessions and institutions are exposed as limiting and contingent, but nothing else exists to take their place. Hence they are simultaneously exposed as necessary. Shakespeare's tragedies fundamentally alter this configuration:

> Shakespeare will compel us to consider our forms of worldly inheritance, on which we have depended in order to live together meaningfully at all, as insufficient, fragmented, weakened, or damaged. The activities that upheld

and affirmed prior modes of social organization – burying
the dead, military service, or courtly speech – will give way,
as we proceed, to activities that break and destroy bonds
on which we, in our lives together as individuals, rely, cul-
minating with acts of torture.[2]

Early modern tragedy *also* exposes the terrifying contingency
of our social relations and customs. Outside or beyond a
sacral order, the customs which bind our lives to one another
(burying the dead, military service, courtly speech) are
exposed as limiting, but their necessity can no longer be reaf-
firmed. According to Kottman, this gives way to greater acts
of cruelty and violence because to find oneself marginalised
in such a makeup is to suffer one's tragic fate absolutely and
irreversibly. The social order as is is exposed not as necessarily just, but as contingently unjust – marginalising for no
good reason whatsoever.

   Contrary to what Steiner might say, the inexorability of
tragedy, hence tragedy itself, is felt more perniciously in a
conception of the cosmos and the passage of time that moves
away from ritual. In order for tragedy to mean, it has to
mean in terms of what it reveals in future. The present suffering of it to no perceivable or calculable end isolates the
tragic protagonist in his suffering in a far more alienating
fashion. Hamlet suffers his particular tragedy in this way.
He suffers the contingency of the unverified until death. To
consider *The Winter's Tale* as indeed 'post-tragic' means to
consider here what the inexorable, irreversible onset of early
modern tragedy entails, particularly if the tragic protagonist
manages to survive its occurrence with his life intact. Once
again, here is Laroque:

The point is no longer to lay the foundations for some
monarchical or imperial enterprise nor to rally energies dis-
sipated amid the din and merrymaking of festivity to serve

in some noble conquest. What now is at stake is the regeneration of the world destroyed by jealousy and a mad lust for power. In the plays of Shakespeare's last period, history, having done away with magical thinking and its train of traditions, deemed to be costly and useless, is apparently struck by impotence and sterility and stuck in an impasse. Thus King Leontes' Sicily, a pastoral land if ever there was one, becomes a wasteland. Now it is in the children lost or exiled far afield, long penitence and the magic of art of old rural rituals that lie the youth and hope of a world made sick by violence.[3]

Laroque deftly establishes the trajectory of historical movement that *The Winter's Tale* depicts. The play depicts 'history' at an impasse and Laroque suggests that the way forward is, in many ways, retrograde – a return to the 'magic of art of old rural rituals' in which lies the only hope for 'a world made sick by violence'. If the first three acts of *The Winter's Tale* depict the unfolding of early modern tragedy, the last two depict a type of recovery, *but not progress*.

The rush of the present is particularly bracing in the play's first three acts. Several contradictory possibilities are taken up, and, just as quickly, lost. Possibilities, at least for Leontes and Paulina, are realised, lost and reclaimed. Leontes suddenly rails like a madman, and then, just as suddenly, is subdued. Paulina is initially firm and straight to the point in her dealings with Leontes. She subsequently relents, not in the content of her message, but in the manner of its delivery.

First, Leontes: he is convinced, beyond any doubt, that Hermione is unfaithful, that the child she bears is not his. At the end of Act 2, scene 1, he not only sends for the oracle, but is convinced that it will corroborate what he knows to be true:

> Though I am satisfied, and need no more
> Than what I know, yet shall the oracle
> Give rest to th'minds of others, such as he
> Whose ignorant credulity will not
> Come up to th' truth.   (2.1.191–5)

This is an astonishing demonstration not of Leontes's magnanimity, but of his assuredness. Hermione is unsure what the oracle will say and does not take it as given that the oracle will sort any of this out to her liking. After the officer reads out her arraignment (prior to revealing the oracle's verdict), Hermione says

> Since what I am to say must be but that
> Which contradicts my accusation, and
> The testimony on my part no other
> But what comes from myself, it shall scarce boot me
> To say 'not guilty'. Mine integrity,
> Being counted falsehood, shall, as I express it,
> Be so received. But thus: if powers divine
> Behold our human actions, as they do,
> I doubt not then but innocence shall make
> False accusation blush and tyranny
> Tremble at patience.   (3.2.20–30)

Hermione does not say, briefly, as Leontes does, 'I am satisfied.' Rather, she braces herself at court for the possibility that the oracle will rule against her. What hindsight bears out is that he who knows, who has every faith in the oracle, is proven false, while she who doubts, who has lesser faith in the oracle, is proven true.

Without the oracle, we as readers would have no way of knowing whether Hermione or Leontes is correct. With it, we marvel more at Leontes's prior conviction and Hermione's lack of conviction. Moreover, we can only further marvel at Leontes's express and casual dismissal of the oracle. He says with hardly any disturbance: 'There is no truth at all i'the'oracle. / The sessions shall proceed. This is mere falsehood' (3.2.138–9). The question worth posing, particularly in our godless, post-sacral order, is: how do *we* know the oracle is correct? The oracle is not exactly a paternity test. *What if the oracle is false?* Again, we come to know that the oracle is correct not because we have grounds to believe it, but because, like Hamlet, Leontes mediates how we are to read the oracle (as ultimately true). But Leontes does not believe the oracle *immediately*. He only believes it once Mamillius dies, which suggests that the price of Leontes's conversion, which we require in many respects to make the play morally intelligible, is the death of his son. Had Leontes continued to insist, despite Mamillius's death, that the oracle was false, nothing, ostensibly speaking, would have changed. His queen and son would still be dead, his child still lost. The conditions for him to renege on his original scepticism would still exist and the play would be, could be, about his *gradual* conversion to the oracle's truth over the next sixteen years. Mamillius's death does not guarantee or necessitate Leontes's conversion to the oracle's truth. That his conversion occurs immediately, in fact, saves us the painful task of asking how we know the oracle is true at all. Put another way: without Mamillius's death, and despite our position outside of the text as readers, we would have no way of convincing Leontes that he is wrong. We would be back in the realm of contingency armed with no clear and discernible way of combating his tyranny.

However deep our criticism goes in posing and seeking to answer such a question, none can ever derive the *necessity* of Leontes's conversion. Upon what, then, do we base our knowledge of the oracle's veracity? The question bears on Leontes's intelligibility, particularly in Hegelian terms. We have two radically different versions of Leontes: one where he is stubbornly obdurate, another where he is profoundly repentant. We also have two radically different versions of Paulina: one where she is acerbic and direct ('I'll use that tongue I have. If wit flow from't / As boldness from my bosom, let't not be doubted / I shall do good' (2.2.55–7)) and another where she is similarly remorseful. After a lord chastises her 'boldness of … speech' (3.3.216), she relents: 'I am sorry for't. / All faults I make, when I shall come to know them, / I do repent' (3.3.216–18). Finally, we have two radically different versions of Hermione: one where she is flesh, another where she is stone – Hermione in death and in life; and if one version of Hermione necessarily cancels out the other, the question is whether we have a right to *expect* some version of intelligibility or consistency from the characters before us. Both Leontes and Paulina hold radically different subjectivities within what we take to be the same bodies. How or in what way does housing such stark possibilities within the same subjectivity speak to, or against, a notion of tragic fate?

Let us return to Hegel here and his discussion of what constitutes a fate. Though here he is not speaking about tragedy, his notion of fate no doubt bears on his particular conception of tragedy. He notes that 'a fate appears to arise through another's deed'.[4] Through interaction with another, one of perhaps any number of possibilities inherent in a character is brought into actuality. So the possibility realised is, indeed, in some sense, the 'true' one and the beginning of a fate. Hegel begins:

> What really produces [a fate] is the manner of receiving and reacting against the other's deed. If someone suffers an unjust attack, he can arm and defend himself and his right, or he may do the reverse. It is with his reaction, be it battle or submissive grief, that his guilt, his fate, begins.[5]

Yet what we have in the case of Leontes is an expression, or a coming to be, of *two* distinct possibilities. Leontes both defends himself and his right and does the reverse in committing to submissive grief. He has at once initiated a fate and negated it. Hegel continues:

> In neither case does he suffer punishment; but he suffers no wrong either. In battle he clings to his right and defends it. Even in submission he does not sacrifice his right; his grief is the contradiction between recognizing his right and lacking the force actually to hold onto it; he does not struggle for it ... Courage, however, is greater than grieving submission, for even though it succumbs, it has first recognized this possibility [of failure] and so has consciously made itself responsible for it; grieving passively, on the contrary, clings to its loss and fails to oppose it with strength. Yet the suffering of courage is also a just fate, because the man of courage engages with the sphere of might and right. Hence the struggle for right, like passive suffering, is an unnatural situation in which there lies the contradiction between the concept of right and its actuality.[6]

In Hegel's account, what is 'right' never changes – simply one's reaction in face of it. The conversion Hegel is discussing is not the refiguration of right, but the refiguration of the reaction to (and even deferral of) the right. What constitutes the right constitutes a fate. This outward antagonism 'between the concept of right and its actuality' is key to Hegel's account of dialectical unfolding – in particular, to his insistence on the sort of inner consistency of (tragic) character which then marks a tragic fate. Leontes's conception of 'right', however, fundamentally changes. First Hermione is absolutely guilty, then she is absolutely innocent. In altering his conception of right, Leontes is taking steps to alter his fate. Can one *alter* one's fate? Leontes in fact initiates not a fate but suffering. He achieves something like a transcendence of his own fate through suffering.

> Unhappiness may become so great that his fate, the self-destruction, drives him so far toward the reunification of life that he must withdraw into the void altogether. But, by himself setting an absolutely total fate against himself, the man has *eo ipso* lifted himself above fate entirely.[7]

Note that above, Hegel is talking not about tragedy, but a move beyond it, the sort a tragic character does *not* achieve. A tragic character achieves his (tragic) fate, usually through death, and does not transcend it. According to Hegel, Leontes (at least a later Leontes, the one who alters his conception of the right) is not a tragic character. By mourning not in the world of action, Leontes's 'fate', in a way, is not really a 'fate', or not a tragic fate. Tragedy can be – in Leontes's case, has been – transcended.

Leontes achieves a Hegelian 'second-order negation', or a 'negation of the negation', which, as Jennifer Bates tells us, 'means that the alienation initiated by the first negation is overcome in a positive resolution'.[8] The first negation is simply the elementary recognition that appearances in the world are not what they seem – for example, Edmund's recognition that the stars do not really control human fates ('This is ... excellent foppery') – hence an expression of a certain type of agency rooted in the self. Leontes similarly negates the oracle's verdict (first order) but then reneges on his original negation (second order). Leontes seems to be, by choosing to suffer passively, taking steps to avoid tragedy. The first-order negation initiates a tragedy, the second a type of suffering that initiates its eventual, but not necessary, transcendence.

According to Hegel (and subsequently, Bradley), only a character who pursues a life of action suffers tragedy.

A character who realises or is willing to make a second-order negation to pursue a life of inaction is not suffering tragedy. But what about a character who achieves a second-order negation but must, for whatever reason, *still commit to action*? The tragedy which ensues is no longer a matter of inner necessity. Now, what has happened instead is that the character, fully understanding and willing to make a second-order negation, will go on to suffer not because of inner necessity, but because of outer contingency. Macbeth suffers in this way. Through action he plays out a second-order negation, though what results is not a positive resolution. In a Hegelian conception, Macbeth does not suffer a fate, but succumbs to tragedy. Leontes, on the other hand, transcends tragedy, but suffers a fate.

Hegel acknowledges the possibility of contradiction within a subjectivity (both A and ~A), but notes that in action, one possibility *must* emerge to the negation of the other. Counterfactual criticism, however, isolates not the dialectical necessity of how either A or ~A came to be, but an understanding that both A and ~A are possible now, in the present. Macbeth does not express some inner necessity of his as true. The truth of his tragedy is that he could have done either A or ~A. Leontes, in fact, achieves, acts out, *both* A and ~A. And the best schematic conception of this insight comes not from Hegel, but from Frye in his discussion of metaphor. Isolating the move of literature (both poetry and criticism) from an 'archetypal phase'[9] to an 'anagogic phase',[10] Frye notes that

> [i]n the anagogic aspect of meaning, the radical form of metaphor, 'A is B', comes into its own. Here we are dealing with poetry in its totality, in which the formula 'A is B' may be hypothetically applied to anything, for there is no metaphor, not even 'black is white', which a reader has any right to quarrel with in advance. The literary universe,

therefore, is a universe in which everything is potentially identical with everything else. This does not mean that any two things in it are separate and very similar, like peas in a pod, or in the slangy and erroneous sense of the word in which we speak of identical twins. If twins were really identical they would be the same person. On the other hand, a grown man feels identical with himself at the age of seven, although the two manifestations of this identity, the man and the boy, have very little in common as regards similarity or likeness. In form, matter, personality, time, and space, man and boy are quite unlike. This is the only type of image I can think of that illustrates the process of identifying two independent forms.[11]

Metaphor, in saying something like 'black is white', has the opportunity to say that a thing is equal to its opposite, not 'A is B' per se, but A = ~A, particularly in a universe where 'everything is potentially identical with everything else'. The consideration of lost possibilities in Shakespeare criticism is to promote an anagogic turn in literary studies. In Hegel's conception, everything is (or can be) both A and ~A *over time*. In the moment, either A or ~A (necessarily) suffices. Yet Frye's conception of the anagogic literary universe gives primacy to both A and ~A *in the present*.

Moreover, in the vast dialectical unfolding that Hegel champions, the antagonism between A and ~A ultimately leads us to something else, its eventual synthesis in B. Neither A nor ~A has any meaning now, but only, ultimately, in relation to something else that does not yet exist, which it becomes the philosopher's or literary critic's lot to uncover. In thinking about renewing social bonds in pre-Hegelian, 'sacred' time, allowing something to clash with itself or its opposite reveals the necessity of one over the other, *but not the vanquishing of that other*. In Hegel's historical, dialectical view, if A = ~A, it is only in relation to B.

Furthermore, it is not only that because B follows A, A caused B (a logical fallacy), but also that B, speaking strictly from a consideration of value, *is better than A*, oft reiterated as the historical discovery of more freedom, or greater degrees of it. Both A and ~A are meaningless in and of themselves. Either gains meaning in relation to B, so in the end, all we have left to renew social bonds is a conception of B that has yet to come into being. This means that in the present, the passage of time is all we have to renew social bonds that stand dissolved. The renewal of communal bonds is eternally *deferred*. Moreover, our rabid desire to formulate B has us continually *denying* the other, the contingent, for the sake of establishing necessity. Nothing means in the present, only in relation to the future, which can only be established by looking to the past. However, if one is hesitant to assert or subordinate meaning to the passage of time, one could do worse than to revisit Frye's conception of things, because what his anatomy achieves is the *detemporalisation of the dialectic*. Frye's conflation of man and boy speaks to this. However or whatever we uncover (or rather discover) to be A and its opposite, all possibilities exist now and do not depend on the dialectical unfolding of events in time. The desire not to subordinate meaning to the passage of time is why Leontes, intuitively, must mourn the loss of Hermione. To do so is not to hope that one day his community will be reconstituted around her (and them together), for *how* could he possibly hope for such a thing? Rather, by holding on to his grief, Leontes is asserting that what is meaningful to him now is not worth sacrificing to the passage of time. He creates the conditions (thematically speaking) necessary for Hermione's resurrection, which requires committing to the belief that her life (hence her death) means something not just now, but always – for him, and for the state over which he presides.

CLEOMENES. Sir, you have done enough, and have performed
A saintlike sorrow. No fault could you make
Which you have not redeemed – indeed, paid down
More penitence than done trespass. At the last,
Do as the heavens have done: forget your evil.
With them, forgive yourself.
LEONTES. Whilst I remember
Her and her virtues, I cannot forget
My blemishes in them, and so still think of
The wrong I did myself, which was so much
That heirless it hath made my kingdom and
Destroyed the sweet'st companion that e'er man
Bred his hopes out of.   (5.1.1–12)

A critique of Hegel's idea of *Aufhebung* (translated in Bates as 'sublation')[12] can be found in the disguised Polixenes's exchange with Perdita. Polixenes, interrogating Perdita on why she refuses to plant and grow gillyvors (a crossbreed, to Perdita 'bastards' (4.4.82)) in her garden, thus reasons dialectically:

POLIXENES. ... You see, sweet maid, we marry
A gentler scion to the wildest stock,
And make conceive a bark of baser kind
By bud of nobler race. This is an art
Which does mend nature – change it, rather – but
The art itself is nature.
PERDITA. So it is.
POLIXENES. Then make your garden rich in gillyvors,
And do not call them bastards.
PERDITA. ... I'll not put
The dibble in earth to set one slip of them.   (4.4.92–100)

Rather than accept that something base is to be ennobled through (biological) synthesis, Perdita insists on maintaining the difference. This insistence on difference, on drawing a line between legitimate and bastard plants, is the sort inherited from her father, someone who also rejects bastards. But Leontes's rejection is a rejection of her. Yet Perdita, divorced from her own history, hence from the possibility of herself as a bastard, is free (or more free here) to entrench the difference. This implies that the particular renewal to be achieved in this play ought to come on the renewal, rather than the disavowal, of a societal distinction of bastards as other. Later, at Leontes's court, a gentleman describes Perdita as someone who could potentially renew communal bonds:

> …This is a creature,
> Would she begin a sect, might quench the zeal
> Of all professors else, make proselytes
> Of who she but bid follow.   (5.1.106–9)

But just before this assertion, Paulina chides the gentleman (''Tis shrewdly ebbed / To say you have seen a better' (5.1.102–3)) because, in his praise of Perdita, he cancels out his earlier praise of Hermione, for which the gentleman can only ask 'pardon' (5.1.103). The scandal the gentleman touches on is the possibility not of a state founded on Hermione's living memory, but of the memory of Hermione succeeding to Perdita's presence, in which, or in whom, there is no memory, as far as the state is concerned. In whom, or in what, does the salvation of the state lie – in Hermione's living memory, or Perdita's dead present, or some synthesis of the two?

The ending of *The Winter's Tale* is often taken to be the thematic triumph of love or forgiveness, but it remains to be seen where the forgiveness is. Hermione never offers it. Leontes takes her hand and in the end reaffirms something like the mythical founding (of their love) that will allow his state to carry on. The sum total of his lines to Hermione is the following:

> What? Look upon my brother. Both your pardons,
> That e'er I put between your holy looks
> My ill suspicion. This' your son-in-law
> And son unto the King, whom, heavens directing,
> Is troth-plight to your daughter.   (5.3.148–52)

Leontes asks for pardon, but we do not know if he receives it, if the act of forgiveness is *completed*. It is not completed in the play. Whatever occurs in the final scene between Leontes and Hermione, the oracle is fulfilled. The oracle is fulfilled the moment Perdita is found. Nothing in the oracle suggests or portends Hermione's resurrection. If we are to accept its 'mythical' or 'sacred' qualities as an event, the divorce between its miraculous occurrence and any foreshadow from the oracle is indeed conspicuous. We have all sorts of reasons for supposing the oracle is correct, but no way of knowing.

The oracle can be read much like the prophecies in *Macbeth*; Shakespeare would not have given us either to have us doubt their veracity. The prophecies in *Macbeth* portend the future, which, we noted earlier, makes its unfolding necessary. (In *Hamlet*, we are given testimony about the past, requiring verification.) However, the oracle here rules on the present. Its 'prophetic' portion, occurring in the subjunctive tense ('the King shall live without an heir if that / which is lost be not found' (3.2.133–4)), must come true of necessity. But does its ruling on the present require posterior verification, or is it a priori necessary? Rather banally, we could say that we as readers accept the oracle's veracity on a type of faith. But if *we* know better than to doubt the oracle, what allows Leontes to do so so brazenly? Leontes does not seek to verify that the oracle is false. He simply *knows* it to be false, just as we know it to be true. He takes his first intuition to be more sacred than the oracle's verdict and so is still, even in his original transgression, firmly attached to a sacred order, merely reconceived with himself rather than the gods at the centre. His transgression is less sacrilegious than hubristic.

However, it is not *necessary* (not ever) for Leontes to accept the oracle. He could go on, even in the world of the play, to accept the passage of historical time, subjecting the oracle's ruling to verification. We might even take such an occurrence to be in line with a type of maturity in jurisprudence. If, in the world of the play, sometime over the course of the next sixteen years, such verification proves impossible, or unlikely, he could then make amends for his own rashness by deciding that while the oracle cannot be proven false, *neither can it be proven true*. We all often make amends for our own rash jealousies in this way; it is, in fact, the *only* way to make amends. The trajectory here is not towards affirmation of the oracle as sacred but away from its sacred hold. Now, such a conversion, or reversion, would be a matter of Machiavellian calculation and one can only wonder whether, *such* being the phenomenological and spiritual path taken by Leontes, the stage would indeed be set for Hermione's resurrection.

Committing to this type of knowledge, knowledge of the contingent to be verified in time, however, is itself unbearable.[13] As mentioned earlier, truth (verification) is left breached. Hegel's dialectical antagonism is never resolved in this play. Leontes's intuition rubs up against the oracle. Each cancels the other out. Why should the oracle prevail? Indeed, in some grand dialectical scheme where the power of the sacred is eventually reduced, Leontes's acceptance of the oracle's ruling is *regressive*. Furthermore, we know that Leontes's original doubt in the first Act is hyperbolic. But his acceptance not only of the oracle's ruling, but of

Hermione's resurrection, is equally hyperbolic. If ever there was a time to doubt, it is now, when Paulina calls upon him to believe in something as ludicrous as stone turning to flesh. He accepts the resurrection, again, with little protest. Leontes has reneged on his original sceptical intuitions absolutely. By doing so, by refusing the spiritual baggage of pragmatic rational calculation, he does provide us with some semblance of a happy ending.

In many ways, however, the ending we get is indicative not of a life restored, but of a life, of their lives (Leontes's and Hermione's), lost or spent. Leontes is not filled with redemptive energies upon seeing Hermione restored in stone. He is ashamed that he no longer has the metaphysical strength to conjure up something that might constitute proper acknowledgement:

> LEONTES. I am ashamed. Does not the stone rebuke me
>   For being more stone than it? O royal piece!
>   There's magic in thy majesty, which has
>   My evils conjured to remembrance and
>   From thy admiring daughter took the spirits,
>   Standing like stone with thee.   (5.3.37–42)

Hermione, upon coming back to life, briefly addresses Perdita, but hardly *rejoices*. Both Hermione and Leontes have suffered, have been ravaged by, the passage of time. Rather than transmit the truth of historical time to their children, however, they instead attempt to confer meaning upon their children through suffering. Their willing regression guarantees that this play has meaning, that their lives, the lives of those at court, the life of his state, are meaningful. In their regression and resignation lies the redemption of the state, if only because what they do not transmit to future generations is the contingency of the unverified, a social order eternally breached. The myth of their union, as a type of sacred knowledge unverifiable in time, allows

Perdita and Florizel to love one another freely within a
state founded on Hermione's living memory rather than
Perdita's dead present.

Shakespeare is challenging his readers to accept Hermione's resurrection as fact. Taking such an event to be true
is hardly to commit to the belief that the resurrection of
dead flesh is biologically possible. Yet the will required to
reverse time for the sake of upholding the social order is
as difficult to muster as that, perhaps, required to raise the
dead.[14] However we may shudder at Leontes's initial dismissal of the oracle, the more miraculous achievement is, in
fact, his obdurate acceptance of its verdict, made manifest
through his willingness to suffer the consequences of his
original transgression for, it seems, the remainder of his life.
The only way to comprehend this is not to assume, with the
benefit of hindsight, that the oracle is necessarily correct,
but to ask ourselves how or why we are convinced that the
oracle is correct at all. It is well within Leontes's purview,
at the very least, to make peace with his prior transgression
without upholding the oracle's veracity – to disengage from
its sacred hold and move forward for the health not only of
himself, but, supposedly, of his state. Such an action would
entail the disengagement of his state from its necessary
existence within a pre-established social order, however. It
would be to subject the state and its citizens to the rav-
ages of historical time and contingency, a move that could
be interpreted as progressive and statesmanlike. Leontes
refuses. Why? Why commit to such masochistic undoing
and needless spiritual suffering? Leontes's suffering is not
the dialectical result of having been severely rebuked, but
corresponds to a willingness to commit to a Hegelian 'second-order negation'. Yet such a negation does not result in
a 'positive resolution'. In the end, Leontes stands shamed
before Hermione anyway, more spent and less redeemed.

Because to commit to Hermione's resurrection is to commit to a type of metaphysics of presence, to insist on, rather than dialectically uncover, its necessity. Taken this way, we discover that we haven't yet been overtaken by a world of mass contingency, that we still have will and fortitude and imagination enough to conceive of the necessity of the contingent, that the strictly verifiable is inadequate or unsuitable knowledge.[15]

CHAPTER 6

'WHY INDEED DID I MARRY?': COUNTERFACTUAL THINKING AND *OTHELLO*

Existing in sacred time within a sacred order has its limits. The dialectical pressure to break free from some overarching 'essentialism' is what gives Shakespeare criticism much of its driving impetus today. What are the Edmunds and Iagos, let alone the Hamlets and the Lears, of the world to do finding themselves marginalised in such a setup? If the social order as is is unbearable, the only suitable way forward, it seems, is to commit to suffering in hopes of transcending perceived injustices. Edmund and Iago are hardly thought of as tragic characters. It is hardly tragic that Edmund is a bastard, or that Iago is overlooked for promotion. Yet neither is willing simply to yield to the 'static' unfolding of sacred time. Each rejects the status quo, choosing instead to exploit his existence in historical time in hopes of manipulating or transforming the social order to achieve not a transcendence of fate, but a conquest of it. This is the meaning behind Edmund's aside: the 'excellent foppery' of the world is one that takes the social order to be necessary, as though human desires are ultimately incapable of transforming it. Iago's advice to Roderigo to 'make money' (1.3.348–9) is a plea to take hold of time. Edmund and Iago believe the dialectic of historical time will reveal not the necessity of their suffering, but rather, their possible liberation. We castigate them as villains for thinking this way, but they are no different from Macbeth when he says that 'time and the hour runs through the roughest day' (1.4.146), which is an elaborate way of saying that time heals all wounds. This is not a Machiavellian sentiment *necessarily*, particularly if the idea is simply that what we are made to suffer can be changed. In a dialectical conception of unfolding, the marginalisation and even possible devastation at the hands of an existing finite social order are not something to be yielded to in the present, but something to be overcome, resulting not in the renewal of social bonds but in their future transmutation. The will to achieve such transmutation, then, is equivalent to curbing tragedy's power in human affairs, and mirrors critical attempts to establish the necessity of tragedy, because the implicit assumption of such criticism is that if we establish suitable reasons why such and such a tragic event occurred, all of us can live to fight another day. What I will attempt to show in this reading of *Othello* is that existence in historical time, while offering a way of surviving tragedy, at the same time trivialises both tragedy and existence.

Listen to Iago's dialectical reasoning. Roderigo, full of angst that the love of his life, Desdemona, has married the Moor, is on the verge of ending his supposedly 'tragic' existence. Iago consoles him thus:

> Come, be a man. Drown thyself? Drown cats and blind puppies ... I say, put money in thy purse. It cannot be long that Desdemona should continue her love to the Moor – put money in thy purse – nor he his to her. It was a violent commencement in her, and thou shalt see an answerable sequestration – fill thy purse with money. The food that to him now is as luscious as locusts shall be to him shortly as bitter as coloquintida. She must change for youth; when she

is sated with his body, she will find the error of her choice.
She must have change, she must. Therefore put money in
thy purse.　　　　　　　　　　　　(1.3.330–44)

Nor is it too much to imagine that 'honest' Iago follows his
own advice, that he reasons similarly when the fates turn
against him. His plot to 'abuse Othello's ears' (2.1.377) is
related to his being overlooked for promotion. What Iago
also despises about Othello, however, is his presence – a
certainty and assuredness in himself impervious to dialectical logic:

> IAGO. Three great ones of the city
> In personal suit to make me his lieutenant,
> Off-capped to him; and by the faith of man,
> I know my price, I am worth no worse a place.
> But he, as loving his own pride and purposes,
> Evades them with a bombast circumstance
> Horribly stuffed with epithets of war,
> Nonsuits my mediators. For, 'Certes', says he,
> 'I have already chose my officer.'　　　　(1.1.8–16)

Since Othello has managed to achieve a type of standing at
court not through the manipulation of words, but through
their more resounding delivery, all the more reason for Iago
to hate him.

Iago, in comparison, is unable to command words to
achieve the sort of standing he believes he deserves (as he
says, 'I know my price'). When he hears the officers on their
way to confront Othello for eloping with Desdemona, Iago
is not inclined to stand and make his case. His first impulse is
to retreat. He advises Othello to do the same:

> IAGO. Those are the raisèd father and his friends.
> You were best go in.　　　　　　　　(1.2.29–30)

But Othello extends his majestic presence:

> OTHELLO. Not I. I must be found.
>   My parts, my title, and my perfect soul
>   Shall manifest me rightly.   (1.2.30–2)

Othello goes on to defuse the scandal at court not by weighing costs and benefits in dialectical or utilitarian fashion, but by being direct. He is charged to 'say it' (1.3.126), to tell how he and Desdemona came to wed. Despite being accused of witchcraft and trickery, he does so with astonishing poise and candour:

> OTHELLO. She loved me for the dangers I had passed,
>   And I loved her that she did pity them.
>   This only is the witchcraft I have used.   (1.3.166–8)

After which there is little left to say. Othello has achieved standing as Desdemona's husband not by skirting or circumventing perceived social infelicities, but by confronting them directly.

Othello's bold words immediately discredit the Duke's. Earlier, he had promised Brabantio, upon hearing that his daughter had married without her father's consent, to throw the entire 'bloody book of law' (1.3.62) at the perpetrator, even were he 'our proper son' (1.3.69). Now, his authority diminished somewhat by Othello's presence, the Duke must proceed more carefully in his counsel:

> Let me speak like yourself, and lay a sentence
> Which, as a grece or step, may help these lovers
> Into your favor.
> When remedies are past, the griefs are ended
> By seeing the worst, which late on hopes depended.
> To mourn a mischief that is past and gone

Is the next way to draw new mischief on.
What cannot be preserved when fortune takes,
Patience her injury a mock'ry makes.
The robbed that smiles steals something from the thief;
He robs himself that spends a bootless grief.(1.3.198–208)

Like Leontes, Brabantio has suffered a fate, in this case, betrayal by his daughter. And however well-meaning the Duke's consolation (however humane the advice, that 'time heals all wounds'), Brabantio understands and refuses to trivialise his loss. Like Perdita, he sees through the emptiness of such reasoning and adamantly entrenches the difference.

He bears the sentence well that nothing bears
But the free comfort which from thence he hears,
But he bears both the sentence and the sorrow
That, to pay grief, must of poor patience borrow.
These sentences, to sugar or to gall,
Being strong on both sides, are equivocal.   (1.3.211–16)

The sentence is to suffer 'patience', which hardly lessens Brabantio's sorrow. In the end, such 'advice' is neither helpful nor harmful but 'equivocal'.

What has been exposed is the contingency of a custom which demands that fathers have some say in their daughter's marriage. Moreover, the charge to suffer patiently exposes the fact that there is no *solution* to the problem at hand. The problem is now Brabantio's alone. Brabantio's fate at this point seems irreversible. He could perhaps take the Duke's advice in order to survive the blow, but instead chooses to suffer. By withdrawing as he does, he asserts the truth of a custom on which he has staked his existence as a man. *He* may suffer irreversibly, but he demands that such a custom be not exposed to, or withered away merely due to unforeseen contingencies brought about by, the passage of time.

For Brabantio, if it is true that time heals all wounds, so too does time create potential, at every turn, to open all wounds. This type of uncertainty, concomitant with our existence in historical time, may remove the burden of tragedy in the moment. In the long run, however, it stands to dissolve all that is serious, to make all that is fair foul. Claiming one's freedom, or refusing to suffer passively because one can live to fight another day, has consequences. Brabantio, in refusing to trivialise what he takes to be real (i.e. a real 'hurt'), asserts that however social custom may have failed at this moment, to throw it out or invalidate it absolutely would be to throw out a world, a world on which his existence is staked. By choosing to suffer, Brabantio holds out for the possibility that such a transgression can be reversed, if not in his own case, then certainly in those of other fathers who have daughters.

Dialectical unfolding makes all things possible over time, opens up a world of contingencies that have yet to come into being. This could be liberating on the one hand or devastating on the other, introducing into human affairs the possibility of a type of dialectical sickness in thought. This sort of sickness is what Othello, in being made to doubt Desdemona's faithfulness, succumbs to. We could point to Iago and suggest that he, who reasons dialectically, infuses Othello with the types of doubts and uncertainties Iago not only thrives on, but gleefully exploits.

What if Iago were no longer a character in the play? Now we cannot seriously entertain such a possibility without making the play wholly unintelligible. Yet Iago himself suggests that the Moor's unmooring is, in a way, destined to happen. Again, consoling Roderigo, Iago says

> [h]er [Desdemona's]eye must be fed; and what delight shall she have to look on the devil? When the blood is made dull with the act of sport, there should be, again to inflame it

and to give satiety a fresh appetite, loveliness in favour, sympathy in years, manners, and beauties – all of which the Moor is defective in. Now, for want of these required conveniences, her delicate tenderness will find itself abused, begin to heave the gorge, disrelish and abhor the Moor. Very nature will instruct her in it and compel her to some second choice.   (2.1.220–9)

Iago makes no mention of himself! 'Very nature' will instruct Desdemona to tire of the Moor for reasons including but not limited to their difference in age ('sympathy in years') and 'loveliness in favour ... manners, and beauties'. Othello himself knows he is direct in speech, hence lacks what others perceive to be social graces. When the sickness begins to take hold, Othello ponders these two *exact* reasons, despite the fact that Iago has uttered not a word of them to him.

> ... If I do prove her haggard,
> Though that her jesses were my dear heartstrings,
> I'd whistle her off and let her down the wind
> To prey at fortune. Haply, for I am black
> And have not those soft parts of conversation
> That chamberers have, or for I am declined
> Into the vale of years – yet that's not much –
> She's gone. I am abused, and my relief
> Must be to loathe her. Oh, curse of marriage,
> That we can call these delicate creatures ours
> And not their appetites!   (3.3.264–74)

Othello has some power to reason exactly as Iago does. He knows he is 'black' (not 'fair' in conversation) and that he is 'declined / Into the vale of years'. Moreover, Cavell's reading of Othello– that Desdemona's possible infidelity is a convenient lie to cover something he knows (in this case that he is 'black', that he is her senior and that these are limitations on him) – resonates in these lines as well.[1] Othello cannot command Desdemona's appetites. In the unfolding of time, what he takes to be his possession of her is subject to the contingencies of her desire.

Yet are we now convinced (1) that Desdemona *will* tire of the Moor and (2) that it is indeed unwise for the Moor to place his life upon her faith? To commit to (1) is to commit to a world ruled not by the resoluteness of our desires, but by their fickleness. It is to ally ourselves, in a way, with Iago's reasoning. And though we might try to put a stop to ill suspicions, *our* thought is nonetheless launched on a dialectical trajectory. Othello tries to will away his suspicions:

> If she be false, oh, then heaven mocks itself!
> I'll not believe't.   (3.3.282–3)

But as we know with the benefit of hindsight, in a world of historical time where all things are possible, the dialectical sickness has already taken hold.

Othello seems doomed to suffer a fate at the hands of Desdemona, who seems equally doomed to tire of Othello. But nothing Desdemona does in the world of this play ever compromises the nature of her devotion to Othello. In fact, Cavell alludes to her perfect obedience to Othello despite even his heinous accusations:

> Though Desdemona no more understands Othello's accusation of her than, in his darkness to himself, he does, she obediently shares his sense that this is their final night … This shows in her premonitions of death (the Willow Song, and the request that one of the wedding sheets be her shroud) and in her mysterious request to Emilia, ' … tonight / Lay on my bed our wedding sheets' (IV, ii, 106–7), as if knowing, and faithful to, Othello's private dream of

her, herself preparing the scene of her death as Othello ... imagines it must happen ... as if knowing that only with these sheets on their bed can his dream of her be contested.[2]

Desdemona, in perfect devotion to her husband, understands that in order to contest his deranged dream of her, she must hope beyond hope that he will see in her her total faithfulness, even at risk of her life. She cannot renege on her love for Othello because it is on her love that she has staked her existence. To renege on that would be to renege on everything she holds dear in the world she inhabits. She, like her father, is willing to suffer for her beliefs.

If we follow Cavell's reading, that Othello is, after all, infinitely separate from Desdemona, we are asking Othello to renege on the possibility of perfect union with Desdemona. Cavell's reading, that is, dooms Othello in a different way. It dooms Othello, and human beings generally, to an existence separate from others. Despite even Cavell's recognition that Othello has no good reason to doubt Desdemona's faithfulness, what he must do, nonetheless, is make peace with her separateness from him. Desdemona does nothing to invite an understanding that she is separate from him. Rather, she tempts him with the possibility of their perfect union, a union upon which she has staked her life just as Othello has. Othello, in short, must be tempted by union with an other, an other who *is* totally devoted to him, and at the same time wilfully deny the possibility of that union. Othello may be better off coming to terms with the notion that the world is beyond his grasp. But should Desdemona do the same? If the realisation that human beings are separate comprises some bit of human knowledge, it seems inhuman of *her* to tempt Othello otherwise. What ought a man to do under such temptation? Should he sagaciously deny the possibility of union between human beings, or take pains all the more stridently to accept his vulnerability and love, wholly, fully, an other – thereby asserting, or at least believing, that the union of two souls is eminently *possible*?

The question is whether love between two souls is a suitable mythology, metaphysic, presence or starting point from which to extract meaning and purpose in *this* world. What is at stake is a cultural orientation not to a world in which everything there is is on display to be discovered, but to one in which something like the perfect love between two souls is achievable, even if shrouded in mystery. We saw in the previous chapter how such considerations factor into the reconciliation of Leontes and Hermione. Leontes's faith and steadfastness in loss bring Hermione back to life. Even if theirs is an 'unhappy' reconciliation, there is mystery enough for the myth of a possible perfect union to be derived from the particular makeup of their final union. Moreover, such a myth is entirely useful in helping to cheer, or make meaningful, the lives of those who live in the state. In such a way is meaning transmitted to others – meaning which, if not empirically unverifiable, then certainly is not empirically verifiable.

Othello voices two options. Like Brabantio, he could suffer his tragic fate by 'whistl[ing]her off and let[ting]her down the wind / To prey at fortune', or, alternatively, pout over his loss: '[Y]et that's not much – / She's gone. I am abused, and my relief / Must be to loathe her.' In either case, Othello registers the veritable pain of his possible betrayal by calling up his passions – either passionately lamenting Desdemona's departure, or angrily loathing her. Either reaction requires significant spiritual stamina. A third option would be to take steps to circumvent any possible betrayal in future. No single act could remove completely the possibility of Desdemona's betrayal, except, of course, murder. This is the option Othello ultimately chooses, an act which, however deranged, preserves the myth of their love as real:

...When I have plucked thy rose,
I cannot give it vital growth again;
It needs must wither...
Be thus when thou art dead, and I will kill thee,
And love thee after.   (5.2.13–19)

Time has stopped. Desdemona can no longer wither. And Othello's mind has been freed of dialectical suspicions.

But clearly the third option is the most morally grotesque. That leaves the first two. Yet the first two take it as a matter of necessity that Desdemona *will* betray Othello. Again, we have no reason to believe that she would. If the lesson of this tragedy is for Othello (and human beings more generally) to accept finitude in face of Desdemona's (or another's) infinite desires (hence that other's infinite separateness from us), we seem committed to a reading that caricatures Desdemona's faithfulness on the one hand, and the fickleness of human desire on the other. We could appeal to all sorts of 'conventions' here – for example, to a dramatic convention that necessarily hollows out Desdemona's character, as though she must be rather one-dimensional in her speech. Shakespeare thus presents her devotion to Othello hyperbolically only to increase the dramatic or tragic resonance at play's end. The veritable union between separate human beings is not a possibility worth considering, never *actually* achievable for either Othello or Desdemona. Yet this denigrates the ideal, if less the veritable truth, of holy matrimony, one in which two souls *do* become one flesh. What sorts of meanings are lost if this ideal, this possibility, is abandoned?

Othello tries to will away his doubts, to commit to a metaphysical union which, for all we know, Desdemona equally shares. But the passage of time cannot be willed away. Contingencies abound. If Othello cannot confront them, prospects are slim for us to do otherwise. The trade-off is between suffering the world for the sake of meaning, or trivialising it for the sake of survival. And if, as Susan Sontag says, tragedy is indeed an 'ennobling vision of nihilism',[3] the seemingly pointless suffering of the individual to no easily quantifiable or calculable end is necessary in order to ennoble not nihilism per se, but human existence.

The best case would have been for Othello to commit fully to loving Desdemona, which means having loved her despite whatever she may or may not have done to him. This first option, to allow Desdemona to 'prey at fortune' (if she does prove unfaithful), as Brabantio does, is given cursory consideration and then just as quickly abandoned: 'yet that's not much – / She's gone. I am abused.' What Othello cannot face is the possibility of mourning, of suffering, her loss. Now it will be said that Othello suffers anyway, not her loss, but anger, jealousy, madness, in the thought of her *possible* loss. Hence Othello has invested too much in Desdemona's faithfulness to him. Were he simply to curb his passions somewhat, he could carry on loving Desdemona and be less susceptible to the 'green-eyed monster'. Friar Laurence's advice to Romeo seems apt here:

> These violent delights have violent ends,
> And in their triumph die like fire and powder.   (2.5.9–10)

It is easy enough, of course, when things end so poorly for Romeo and Juliet, then to say that their passions all along were misguided. Perhaps violent delights indeed have violent ends. Both Romeo and Juliet suffer a fate. Both are willing to suffer the consequences of their passions (at the very least, both indubitably *do* suffer the consequences). But Othello is unwilling to suffer the consequences of love, yet all too willing to suffer the consequences of jealousy. Why? To say he doesn't have a choice in the matter is to ignore his own repression of choice ('yet that's not much'). Othello *chooses* not to suffer, as does Iago. Othello intuits that the sacred order as is could very well lead to his loss of standing. No mastery of social convention can guarantee the *impossibility* of such a loss. Iago survives this knowledge by moving away, dialectically, from the power of the sacred. But unlike Iago, Othello remains enamoured by it and demands that the world still have meaning. The dialectical sickness is particularly pernicious for Othello because of these competing psychical demands. Othello cannot face what Iago faces constantly: first, the possible loss of standing at court, and second, the possibility that words are meaningless, and hence so too the world. Again, Iago is not a tragic character. He survives his fate by living to fight another day. When Cassio frets over his loss of standing, Iago's tone is virtually indistinguishable from the one used earlier to console Roderigo:

> IAGO. Come, you are too severe a moraler. As the time, the place, and the condition of this country stands, I could heartily wish this had not befallen; but since it is as it is, mend it for your own good.   (2.3.278–81)

Roderigo, Cassio or even Desdemona (2.1.144–5): Iago counsels each effectively not via flattery, but by chronicling 'small beer' (2.1.162) – i.e. via trivialisation.

The only way for Othello to liberate himself from the possible loss of standing is to turn the problem of Desdemona's faithfulness into an intellectual problem to be solved (the handkerchief). Othello must extricate himself from any possible static thinking that reduces his standing in court and instead put his thoughts in motion, to 'dialecticise' them in a way by proposing a proposition to be verified or refuted in time. Where Cavell believes that Othello's tragedy is rooted in his insatiable desire for a perfect union, I would argue that the loss of the possibility of a perfect union is what leads to Othello's 'self-consuming disappointment' and 'world-consuming rage'.[4] The myth of a perfect union, temporarily breached, *must be restored*. To 'accept finitude', or one's eternal separateness from an other (the oft-repeated 'lesson' of Cavell's views on tragedy), is to commit to a universe in which meaning is continually deferred, verification left breached eternally, which carries its own pitfalls and limitations. Perhaps perfect union is unattainable; it is certainly not verifiable now or in the future. Yet its possibility must continue to be striven for, which means brought to bear (suffered) in the present.

We seem, strangely, to have returned to an old-fashioned critical championing of 'suffering', the sort of aesthetic lesson from which a type of historicist or materialist criticism is thought to have redeemed us. Marx's adage, for example, that the point of philosophy is not merely to interpret the world, but to change it, reorients not only the function of philosophy, but that of criticism, and even tragedy for that matter. Jonathan Dollimore, from a cultural materialist perspective, has this to say about the humanist tendency to reify suffering:

> [T]he humanist view of Jacobean tragedies like *Lear* has been dominant, having more or less displaced the explicitly Christian alternative. Perhaps the most important distinction between the two is this: the Christian view locates man centrally in a providential universe; the humanist view likewise centralizes man but now he is in a condition of tragic dislocation: instead of integrating (ultimately) with a teleological design created and sustained by God, man grows to consciousness in a universe which thwarts his deepest needs ... If that suffering is to be justified at all it is because of what it reveals about man's intrinsic nature –

his courage and integrity. By heroically enduring a fate he is powerless to alter ... man grows in stature even as he is being destroyed.[5]

For Dollimore, the Christian 'providential' view of suffering and a secular humanist view of endurance are merely 'two sides' of the same 'essentialist humanism'.[6] Hence to suppose that the secular humanist view is any sort of break from critical prescriptions of a time gone by is entirely fallacious. For Dollimore, 'existential humanism is merely a mutation of Christianity and not at all a radical alternative'.[7] He proposes a 'materialist reading' in order to separate ourselves from the disempowering vision of tragic suffering, and to assert instead an invigorating notion of 'radical' tragedy that both calls attention to suffering and details, of course, the material conditions for that suffering.

> The notion of a tragic victim somehow alive and complete in death is precisely the kind of essentialist mystification which [King Lear]refuses. It offers instead a decentring of the tragic subject which in turn becomes the focus of a more general exploration of human consciousness in relation to social being – one which discloses human values to be not antecedent to, but rather in-formed by, material conditions.[8]

According to Dollimore, the specific material conditions to consider when reading Lear are those surrounding the nature of 'power, property and inheritance'.[9] Shakespearean tragedy is great not because it depicts tragedy, but because it depicts *why* tragedy, or what *causes* tragedy.

Yet whether New Historicist (in which the stage and the plays are read as suffering from ideological contamination) or cultural materialist (in which the subjective analysis of individual objects creates room for subverting that contaminant), both forms of inquiry are merely opposing sides of the same *dialectical* coin. In reaching for reasons why, Dollimore has succumbed to the same sickness Othello does at line 247 of Act 3, scene 3 ('Why did I marry?'). In both cases, tragedy is construed as a problem to be solved, hence a problem to be overcome *in the future*. Neither Othello nor Dollimore is willing to champion the power of suffering in the present, the power of suffering a world for the sake of meaning, which does not mean passively accepting the world, or injustice, as is. Rather, suffering, so conceived, entails creating, or attempting to create, the conditions for a type of justice to materialise not in some future world, but in some better manifestation of *this* world, on which one has staked one's existence already. An individual may find himself or herself powerless to alter his or her fate. But then to leave the world up to contingencies irreversibly is to create a world, however implicitly, unworthy of transmitting to future generations, because to do so would be to transmit to them the (eventual) realisation of their own powerlessness and triviality. Only by rejecting the world does Brabantio deny nihilism, ennobling it in a way. To concede that the world is ultimately meaningless, that his values and beliefs are ultimately trivial (whether to his daughter or to himself), would be to grant contingency far too much power in human affairs. And while this project has been making a case *for* a consideration of contingencies, it does so as a means of coming to terms with the fact that asserting something like necessity in the face of the contingent is not the only recourse to provide some sort of healthy stability to our criticism. What we have to ask is whether we have the critical strength to resist not the dialectical unfolding of thought per se, but the continual deferral of meaning. The only way to make meaning is not by appealing to some grand methodology or theoretical paradigm, but to let a thousand possibilities and readings flourish in the present, to avoid critical attempts to unify them. Only in so doing can the creative, subversive, even 'radical' element of tragedy materialise. Dollimore wishes no longer to reify suffering. In so doing, he has refused to reify tragedy also and has, like others before him, deferred its meaning to some point in the future. He has allied himself with the Machiavellian proclivities of Iago. Tragedy becomes not 'radical', but all too trivial.

CHAPTER 7

CONCLUSION

I am making the case that Shakespeare criticism is caught in a dialectical trap. In the aggregate, Shakespeare verifies either our freedom or our unfreedom. In the current critical climate, counterfactual thinking could only be read as a type of character criticism, or renewal of Bradleyan character criticism. However, Bradley's 'flaws' are not discovered; they are applied to the text in advance, quashing character freedom. Counterfactual criticism attempts to recover this freedom by emphasising the play of outer contingency over inner necessity. Yet moving forward, no critical law dictates that considering counterfactuals demands the discussion of character over events, as character is no doubt shaped by events anyway. In the matrix of contingencies available in the present, it may *now* be worth emphasising character choice. But the discussion of possible *events* could just as easily lead the conversation of counterfactual thinking. Where character meets event is a contested site, not in presupposing other factors to clash there, but in acknowledging that each exists in juxtaposition to the other. Neither side can be verified as true once and for all. Put simply, a character's freedom is *not* a stable entity or personality trait that said character simply accepts or denies, as though it is our critical lot to establish whether or not he does *that*. Rather, it is to reiterate that just because a character *chooses* does not constitute a fate, which is a negation of choice. A character, of course, *must* choose. Macbeth makes his choice, which is, in his peculiar case, an attempt to negate choice and action, which could have been achieved more readily (but less dramatically) had he chosen to do nothing. But after Macbeth chooses, critics who comment on Macbeth or anyone else after the fact will be tempted to seek out a dangerous sort of knowledge – one that must come up with ways, whether aesthetic, psychological or material, to explain *why* said character chose one way and not another, wanting to believe that by choosing alone, said character has relinquished his freedom. But freedom exists only when possibilities are open. Just because one choice is made over another does not mean that one had to choose that one, out of necessity, over the others. Yet this is the rabbit any propositional criticism will chase out *eternally*.

We discussed in the Introduction the intimate relationship of tragedy to an institution couched in stagnant mythological forces. Rationality, or what Steiner calls 'the myth of reason', renders tragedy survivable because all of us, living within a conception of time in which we are necessarily moving towards something we can conceive as redemptive, corrodes the power of tragedy, radical or destructive or otherwise, by promising the dialectical conquering of it. Hegel conceives of this as a transcendence; in his conception of surviving a fate, one is able (via suffering alone, or only via suffering), as he puts it, 'eo ipso' to overcome a hurt. Hegel is going to some lengths to assert the ability of an individual to achieve something that could be conceived of as redemptive. In some grand dialectical scheme of things, this places the 'right' of the sufferer in its proper dialectical place, which is, in the last instance, supposed to make our perception of that hurt somehow morally palatable. In this conception of suffering, suffering only *means* for reasons that the sufferer himself cannot be aware of. In the immediate present, such suffering is meaningless. But for Leontes, unknowing the future means suffering the present. For critics, suffering the present requires forgoing knowledge of the future.

In what sense exactly are the New Historicism and cultural materialism redemptive? In what way do they presuppose *movement*, what I have here referred to as a type of dialectical unfolding over time, a type of teleology? New Historicism is, in fact, thought to be a type of stagnant criticism, that is, synchronic. Moreover, how indeed could *any* criticism that presupposes the answers in advance be thought of as implying movement *towards* something? Finally, what is meant by teleology, exactly? Is it that our goal-oriented criticism is moving towards something known already which must be uncovered in the texts we read, or that we must increase our knowledge of power relations to reveal something that at present remains concealed? Once again, these are the two poles which straddle all manner of propositional criticism made after the fact. We must either more forcefully apply our historical understanding to verify that our understanding of the nature of power relations is always already everywhere in Shakespeare (New Historicism), or we must uncover in how many ways the knowledge we have has simply been inadequately, or inexhaustively, articulated for the time being (cultural materialism). In the former case, all that is required is a greater *quantity* of verification. In the latter, it is the *quality* of verification that is lacking. Verification now or (ultimate) verification deferred both presuppose a telos: *more* freedom at some point in the future, meaning we have less of it now. We may have our ups and downs, but ultimately, we are getting *somewhere*, and the goal of criticism, while it is to comment on the present, is to be more readily aware of this teleological end goal and ultimately work to bring it about.

This is the sort of dogmatic assumption that counterfactual thinking is an antidote against.[1] I am not saying we are, or should be, getting nowhere. I am saying we cannot possibly know in advance where we are, or ought to be, heading (if anywhere). The true dichotomy to consider is not that between the individual on the one hand and the totalising society on the other, but that between the actual and the possible. Ewan Fernie sets off these opposing poles via Badiou and Derrida:

> After *Specters of Marx*, poststructuralist spirituality seemed for a while to be the only theoretically credible option. But Badiou ... [has] now challenged Derrida in a series of books that has given spirituality a sharper political edge ... Contra Derrida's spirituality of deferral, ... [Badiou] declare[s] ... that 'the impossible happens': that is, it really is possible to bring the beyond into the world *now*.[2]

Without blowing open readings of Shakespeare by both Derrida and Badiou, who are only tangentially interested in Shakespeare anyway, the hope in revitalising Shakespeare studies comes in either allowing his work to point to redemption in the future (Derrida), or in bringing about something we might recognise as liberation immediately (what Fernie calls a spirituality of 'advent'[3]). Obviously, the hope in the former case is that we can know what we are after in advance. In the latter case, we must brace ourselves for what the present *reveals*. The tension is between the gradual dialectical uncovering of meaning established a priori, or an immediate dialectical clash (between what happens and *what does not*) resulting in immanent revelation. Is it *wrong*, morally, spiritually, to strive for the latter, less to use Shakespeare as a cipher aiding us in the long march towards liberation and more to demand from him and his corpus immediate aesthetic revelation, to our liberation possibly, but also, possibly, *to our horror?* If this project is to claim a definition of tragedy, it would be tragedy as the sudden, vicious and visceral realisation that this world is an infinite number of times removed from being the best of all possible worlds. This is an extension of perhaps the more terrifying realisation that our current self is an aberration, nowhere near anything we *know* is our best self, the best of all our possible selves. That our lives make more sense as an aggregate of lost possibilities, rather than as a story describing the necessity of that small sliver of possibility we have managed, for whatever reason, to gain, is the essence of what we might call a tragic vision. To reclaim lost possibilities by considering alternatives is a plea for (the reversal of) time – it is to ask for miracles.[4]

NOTES

Chapter 1

1. His emphasis; Stanley Cavell, *Disowning Knowledge in Seven Plays of Shakespeare* (Cambridge, MA: Cambridge University Press, 2003), p. 93.
2. A.C. Bradley, *Shakespearean Tragedy*, ed. Robert Shaughnessy (1904; New York: Palgrave Macmillan, 2007), p. 12.
3. Ewan Fernie, for example, notes the rise of 'presentism' in Shakespeare studies, which he defines as 'a deliberate strategy of interpreting texts in relation to current affairs, stressing, perhaps, prevailing "presentist" social and cultural interpretations'. Grady and Hawkes, on the other hand, define 'presentism' much more loosely, noting that the term 'presentism' is useful primarily in signalling a break from the past (i.e. historicism): 'We believe that presentist criticism is very much an open-ended and on-going project. Its boundaries remain to be defined.' Ewan Fernie, ed., *Spiritual Shakespeares* (New York: Routledge, 2005), p. 186. Hugh Grady and Terence Hawkes, eds, *Presentist Shakespeares* (New York: Routledge, 2007), p. 5.
4. George Steiner, *The Death of Tragedy* (New York: Knopf, 1961), p. 324.

5. Ibid., p. 324.

6. Cavell, *Disowning Knowledge*, p. 94.

7. Aristotle, *The Poetics*, ed. T.A. Moxon (New York: E.P. Dutton, 1934), p. 16.

8. His emphasis; Northrop Frye, *Anatomy of Criticism* (New York: Atheneum, 1969), p. 49.

9. Terence Cave, *Recognitions: A Study in Poetics* (Oxford: Clarendon Press, 1988), p. 194.

10. George Wilson Knight, *The Wheel of Fire* (London: Oxford University Press, 1930), p. 31.

11. Ibid., p. 32.

12. Ibid., p. 15.

13. Frye, *Anatomy*, p. 119. That the anagogic universe contains the sum total of all possible *anagnorises* points to the infinite number of possible discoveries to be made within a finite conceptual structure. Dante's original use of the term 'anagogy', as the last layer of the four-fold interpretive scaffolding, has the anagogical pointing to the afterlife. In non-eschatological terms, the infinite number of possibilities to be claimed reflects on the infinitude of our desires, any notion of the infinite being otherworldly.

14. *The Norton Shakespeare*, eds, Stephen Greenblatt et al. (New York: W.W. Norton, 1997), pp. 2309–10.

15. Stephen Greenblatt, *Shakespearean Negotiations* (Berkeley: University of California Press, 1988), p. 1.

16. Ibid., p. 2.

17. Ibid., p. 2.

18. Ibid., p. 2.

19. Ibid., p. 7.

20. Ibid., p. 6.

21. Cavell, *Disowning Knowledge*, p. 93.

22. Geoffrey Hawthorn, *Plausible Worlds* (Cambridge: Cambridge University Press, 1991), p. 26.

23. Nassim Nicholas Taleb, *The Black Swan* (New York: Random House, 2007), p. 63.
24. Ibid., p. 63.
25. Daniel Kahneman, *Thinking, Fast and Slow* (Doubleday Canada, 2011), ch. 19.
26. G.W.F. Hegel, *Hegel on Tragedy*, eds Anne Paolucci and Henry Paolucci (Smyrna: Bagehot Council, 2001), pp. 90–1.
27. Cavell, *Disowning Knowledge*, 94.
28. Ibid., pp. 91–2.
29. Ibid., p. 92.
30. Ibid., p. 92.
31. Ibid., p. 92.
32. Ibid., p. 93.
33. Ibid., p. 93.
34. Marjorie Garber, *Shakespeare After All* (New York: Pantheon, 2004), p. 40.
35. David Scott Kastan, '"A rarity most beloved": Shakespeare and the Idea of Tragedy', in *A Companion to Shakespeare's Works*, 4 vols, vol. 1, eds Richard Dutton and Jean E. Howard (Malden: Blackwell, 2003), p. 9.
36. Wilbur Sanders has made note of these very lines before and argues, as Chapter 4 does, that whatever the nature of Macbeth's ambition, it does not 'demand ... murder' – hence suggesting that other options, including bypassing murder altogether, are certainly within Macbeth's purview. See Wilbur Sanders and Howard Jacobson, *Shakespeare's Magnanimity: Four Tragic Heroes, Their Friends, and Families* (Oxford: Oxford University Press, 1978), p. 70.
37. Susan Sontag, *Against Interpretation and Other Essays*, 1966 (New York: Picador, 1996), p. 136.
38. Stephen Booth, *King Lear, Macbeth, Indefinition, and Tragedy* (New Haven: Yale University Press, 1983), p. 84.

39. Steiner, *Death of Tragedy*, p. 321.
40. Terry Eagleton, *Sweet Violence: The Idea of the Tragic* (Oxford: Blackwell, 2003), pp. 94–5.
41. Stanley Cavell, *The World Viewed* (Cambridge, MA: Harvard University Press, 1971), p. 26.
42. Jean E. Howard, 'The New Historicism in Renaissance Studies', in *Shakespeare: An Anthology of Criticism, 1945–2000*, ed. Russ McDonald (Malden: Blackwell, 2004), p. 461.
43. Ibid., p. 469.
44. Ibid., p. 473.
45. Ibid., p. 473.
46. The charge that one must 'historicize new historicism', as Catherine Belsey puts it, is prevalent, though (1) somewhat muted and (2) somewhat unconvincing. For example, James Cunningham notes how 'Stanley Fish sees new historicism as bound to operate within the positivist assumptions that it explicitly opposes' and how 'Fish maintains that without this bracketing off of textuality, historical as opposed to historiographical analysis could not take place.' Moreover, where both Greenblatt and Howard have expressly called for the necessity of acknowledging the present in criticism (or, in Howard's case, calling attention to the 'myth of objectivity' of the past), neither is willing to do so beyond asserting the odd perfunctory bromide. Greenblatt, for example, has said that one's 'voice is important' and that the only way to revitalise much of literary criticism is 'to actually put yourself on the line as somebody'. It is less that the past is a refashioning and more that to make the present is to refashion the past, something which a 'later' Greenblatt is sensitive to. See Catherine Belsey, 'Historicising New Historicism', in *Presentist Shakespeares*, eds Hugh Grady and Terence Hawkes (New York: Routledge, 2007), p. 27; James Cunningham, *Shakespeare's*

Tragedies and Modern Critical Theory (Madison: Fairleigh Dickinson University Press, 1997), pp. 79–80; Stephen Greenblatt, 'Stephen Greenblatt: The Wicked Son', interview by Harvey Blume, *Bookwire* (2001), accessed December 2012.

47. Louis Montrose, 'Professing the Renaissance: The Poetics and Politics of Culture', in *The New Historicism*, ed. H. Aram Veeser (London: Routledge, 1989), p. 23.

48. Neema Parvini, *Shakespeare's History Plays* (Edinburgh: Edinburgh University Press, 2012), p. 17.

49. Neema Parvini, *Shakespeare and Contemporary Theory* (New York: Bloomsbury, 2012), p. 111.

50. Ibid., p. 110.

51. Kiernan Ryan, 'Introduction', in *New Historicism and Cultural Materialism: A Reader*, ed. Kiernan Ryan (London: Arnold, 1996), p. xv.

52. Simon Palfrey, *Shakespeare's Possible Worlds* (Cambridge: Cambridge University Press, 2014), p. 161.

53. Her emphasis; Howard, 'New Historicism', p. 469.

54. Friedrich Nietzsche, *On the Advantage and Disadvantage of History for Life*, trans. Peter Preuss (Indianapolis: Hackett, 1980), p. 11.

55. Ibid., pp. 11–12.

56. Friedrich Nietzsche, *The Birth of Tragedy and the Case of Wagner*, trans. Walter Kaufmann (Toronto: Random House, 1967), p. 46.

57. Nietzsche, *Advantage and Disadvantage*, p. 10.

58. Sarah Beckwith uses this wonderful term, 'post-tragic', to describe the later romances, *Pericles, Cymbeline, The Winter's Tale* and *The Tempest* – a suitable moniker which underscores the notion that these plays thematise questions surrounding what 'surviving' tragedy might entail. Sarah Beckwith, *Shakespeare and the Grammar of Forgiveness* (Ithaca: Cornell University Press, 2011), p. 1.

Chapter 2

1. Bradley, *Shakespearean Tragedy*, p. 15. A slightly altered version of my chapter first appeared as 'My Kingdom for a Ghost: Counterfactual Thinking and *Hamlet*' in *Shakespeare Quarterly* 66.1 (2015): 29–46.
2. Bradley, *Shakespearean Tragedy*, p. 64.
3. Ibid., pp. 64–5. Margreta de Grazia notes that prior to the eighteenth century, the delay was thought not psychologically problematic, but comic. See her *'Hamlet' without Hamlet* (Cambridge: Cambridge University Press, 2007), pp. 172–3. What I am attempting is to remove both the strictly psychological reading of Hamlet's delay and the one that highlights its 'artificial' attributes, comic or otherwise.
4. Bradley, *Shakespearean Tragedy*, p. 72.
5. Most editions of Hamlet conflate parts of the Folio (F) and Quarto 2 (Q2). *The Norton Shakespeare* distinguishes Q2 lines from those of F by using decimal points in line numbering.
6. René Girard, *A Theatre of Envy* (Leominster: Gracewing, 2000), p. 287.
7. W. W. Greg, 'Hamlet's Hallucination', *Modern Language Review* 12 (1917): 393–421.
8. Ibid., p. 396.
9. Ibid., p. 401.
10. Greg recognises that Hamlet utters only four lines in the time between Luciano's pouring of the poison into the Player King's ears and the king's rising – hardly enough time for Hamlet to do all of the things Greg has him do, including 'shouting, gesticulating' and not quite springing at Claudius's throat. Yet Greg, in a note of his own, maintains that such is the only 'legitimate' reading, reminding us that in the following scene and 'elsewhere, it is assumed that it was

Hamlet's behavior, not the King's, that broke up the court'. Ibid., p. 406.

11. Dover Wilson, *What Happens in Hamlet* (Cambridge: Cambridge University Press, 1959), pp. 138–53.

12. At this point, a third scenario is possible: depicting Claudius as both attentive to the play and silent, repressing his alarm (also known as the 'second tooth' theory). Yet such a possibility adds more ambiguity than it removes. Staging Claudius as silent but repressed is as invasive as staging him distracted. To my mind, Greg's reading is still the only one that does not reach for anything more than what is in plain view. Ibid., p. 151.

13. Technically, Marcellus utters the word 'rotten' (1.4.67), but his turn of phrase describes Hamlet's perception of things as well.

14. Bradley, *Shakespearean Tragedy*, p. 88.

15. Greg, 'Hamlet's Hallucination', pp. 413–14.

16. Maynard Mack notes that *Hamlet* 'reverberates with questions', 'immediate riddles' and 'mysteriousness'. He construes the play as a scandal concerning our lack of divine knowledge, while I emphasise the scandalous realisation of our inability to access ordinary human knowledge, knowledge that is readily available to our senses but, somehow, is not. See Maynard Mack, 'The World of Hamlet', in *Shakespeare: The Tragedies: A Collection of Critical Essays*, ed. Alfred Harbage (Englewood Cliffs: Prentice Hall, 1964), pp. 46, 47, 53.

17. Carl Schmitt, *Hamlet or Hecuba: The Irruption of Time into the Play*, trans. Simona Draghici (Corvallis: Plutarch Press, 2006), p. 16.

18. Ibid., p. 17.

19. Eric P. Levy, *'Hamlet' and the Rethinking of Man* (Madison: Fairleigh Dickinson University Press, 2008), p. 126.

20. To account for Hamlet's particular hysteria, it may be wise to remember that his passions are not indicative of

an inner phenomenon exclusively. As Gail Kern Paster reminds us, discussing Shakespearean tragic protagonists in particular, '[t]he passions ... act like winds and tides within and upon the tragic hero because those passions are strong enough to cause changes of mood and disposition in his inward self and hence in his outward behaviour. But such emotions are relational because they cannot be understood by the tragic hero (or by us) apart from the particularized dramatic worlds in which they occur'. See Paster, 'The Tragic Subject and Its Passions', in *The Cambridge Companion to Shakespearean Tragedy*, ed. Claire McEachern (Cambridge: Cambridge University Press, 2002), p. 145.

Chapter 3

1. Kent Cartwright, *Shakespearean Tragedy and Its Double: The Rhythms of Audience Response* (University Park: Pennsylvania State University Press, 1991), p. 9.
2. Ibid., p. 11.
3. Ibid., p. 15.
4. Ibid., p. 16.
5. Ibid., p. 17.
6. Ibid., p. 42.
7. Ibid., p. 41.
8. Ibid., p. 31.
9. Cavell, *Disowning Knowledge*, pp. 103–4.
10. Cavell, *World Viewed*, p. 26.
11. Cartwright, *Shakespearean Tragedy*, p. ix.
12. Ibid., p. 11.
13. Ibid., p. 11.
14. Antonin Artaud, *The Theatre and Its Double*, trans. Mary Caroline Richards (1938; New York: Grove Press, 1958), p. 26.

15. Ibid., p. 48.
16. Ibid., p. 68.
17. Ibid., p. 31.
18. Ibid., p. 52.
19. Ibid., p. 43.
20. Ibid., p. 71.
21. Ibid., p. 47.
22. Ibid., p. 39.
23. Jeffrey Kahan, 'If Only: Alternatives and the Self of King Lear', in *'King Lear': New Critical Essays*, ed. Jeffrey Kahan (New York: Routledge, 2008), p. 356.
24. Northrop Frye, 'King Lear' in *Bloom's Modern Critical Interpretations: 'King Lear'*, ed. Harold Bloom (New York: Bloom's Literary Criticism, 2010), p. 14.
25. Ibid., p. 15.
26. Kahan, 'If Only', p. 355.
27. Samuel Taylor Coleridge, *The Literary Remains of Samuel Taylor Coleridge: Shakespeare, with Introductory Matter on Poetry, the Drama, and the Stage*, ed. Harry Nelson Coleridge (London: William Pickering, 1836), p. 190.
28. Robert Stam, *Reflexivity in Film and Literature: From Don Quixote to Jean-Luc Godard* (New York: Columbia University Press, 1992), p. 4.
29. Bradley, *Shakespearean Tragedy*, p. 286.
30. Coleridge, *Literary Remains*, p. 194.

Chapter 4

1. This is a lukewarm rendition of what Harry Berger Jr does in his reading of *Macbeth*. In lieu of Berger's reading, it is difficult to make the case that it is at precisely this point that Macbeth becomes aware of his position in a hierarchical structure. Berger insists that everyone

in the play is aware of their positions in such a structure from the outset. Even reports by a seemingly disinterested (and unnamed) captain betray this. In his one-sided description of Macbeth's military prowess to Duncan, one can read, prima facie, a laudatory celebration of Macbeth's heroism. Berger cautions us, however, that the captain is simultaneously warning Duncan, precisely by insisting on the lopsidedness of Macbeth's victory, that Macbeth himself is a threat to the crown, and not necessarily a defender of it. 'This warning does not center specifically on Macbeth; it centres generally on the danger of violence, of bloody mindedness which is stimulated and valued in warrior society because essential to its survival. Valor's minions may propel their emulative energies toward rebellion and treachery as well as toward loyal service.' Hindsight, of course, tips the scales of interpretation in favour of 'rebellion and treachery', but the possibility of 'loyal service' remains. (If Duncan's purpose in naming Malcolm his heir is to rebuff Macbeth's advances, why does he then choose to sojourn at Inverness?) Berger wants to trap Macbeth within a warrior society that necessitates he act just as he does. My claim, to the contrary, is that he can consider alternatives. He certainly *does*; he imagines the possibility of doing nothing. In the end, he denies this knowledge and his complicity is redistributed. By emphasising the prevalence of warrior culture, Berger also redistributes complicity. I am, likewise, saying that Macbeth's complicity is redistributed (he is led by outer forces); but it is not a matter of necessity that it be redistributed. To understand Macbeth's tragedy is not to reiterate why things happened the way they did but to isolate where and how they could have happened differently. Marking the distinction speaks to our ability to perceive the tragic effect. The key critical question to ask is not why Macbeth did what he did, but whether or not it is moral or amoral to allow oneself to be led by outer forces at all. Harry Berger, Jr, 'The Early Scenes of *Macbeth*: Preface to a New Interpretation', *English Literary History* 47.1 (1980), p. 10.

2. This marks the trajectory of Bradley's reading of the play, which seeks to establish, definitively, when Macbeth has it in his head to murder Duncan; though rather than delay the possibility, Bradley takes pains to quicken it, concluding that Macbeth had designs on the crown prior to the sisters' prophecy, sealing Macbeth's fate before the play even begins. See Bradley, *Shakespearean Tragedy*, p. 386.

3. Ibid., p. 11.

4. Sianne Ngai, in seeking to establish the dramatic worth of characters who are prone not to action but to 'ugly feelings' (a range of 'negative emotions' that lead not to grand dramatic outward action but to inner passivity and confusion), claims that these feelings nonetheless 'under[write] canonically major forms and genres like Homeric epic and Shakespearean tragedy'. A discussion of negative emotions vis-à-vis the characters of, say, high tragedy is not beyond the pale, though discussion of formal constraints in canonical works tend to focus on 'grander' emotions like 'pity and fear'. Ngai is emphasising competing and contradictory 'feelings' over action, which is, to my mind, a critical embrace of character freedom. See Sianne Ngai, *Ugly Feelings* (Cambridge, MA: Harvard University Press, 2005), pp. 1, 9–10.

5. Cavell does talk about the 'acceptance of the sufficiency of human finitude'. But here his words are meant to prop up the indeterminacy of finitude, hence to commit to a world that places infinite demands on us armed only with finitude, a fate that leaves us

remarkably open to the contingent. Accepting our own finitude does not mean retreating from the world because we can't make sense of it, but means going along in the world and only being able to make partial or piecemeal sense of it – to drown, so to speak, in infinity and attempt to stay afloat. We must have the courage, that is, to face limitlessness, infinitude. See Stanley Cavell, *Must We Mean What We Say?* (Cambridge: Cambridge University Press, 1976), p. 61.

Chapter 5

1. Paul A. Kottman, *Tragic Conditions in Shakespeare* (Baltimore: Johns Hopkins University Press, 2009), p. 21.
2. Ibid., p. 22.
3. François Laroque, *Shakespeare's Festive World: Elizabethan Seasonal Entertainment and Professional Stage*, trans. Janet Lloyd (Cambridge: Cambridge University Press, 1991), p. 208.
4. G.W.F. Hegel, 'The Spirit of Christianity and its Fate', in *Philosophers on Shakespeare*, ed. Paul A. Kottman (Stanford: Stanford University Press, 2009), p. 54.
5. Ibid., p. 54.
6. Ibid., p. 54.
7. Ibid., p. 56.
8. Jennifer Ann Bates, *Hegel and Shakespeare on Moral Imagination* (Albany: SUNY Press, 2010), p. 30.
9. Frye, *Anatomy*, p. 118.
10. Ibid., p. 119.
11. Ibid., pp. 124–5.
12. Bates, *Hegel and Shakespeare*, p. xv.

13. Hegel's account of dialectical unfolding, mirrored in Bradley's insistence that 'deeds are the predominant factor', is essentially tautological because whatever deeds arise, however contradictory in the present, their necessity is established after the fact. Leontes accepts the oracle and thus transcends tragedy. Had he not done so, he might have gone on, as the case is made in this chapter, to be more tempered in his ability to judge events; but he certainly need not accept the oracle. Accepting the oracle, however, allows him to avoid meaninglessness. No one *would* suffer (in Hegelian terms 'transcend') their fate without an immediately present sacral, or communal, order capable of 'ratifying' the legitimacy of the hurt or suffering in question. The 'belief' in an ultimate dialectic unfolding (that one's suffering will make sense to someone at some point) is of no consolation whatsoever. It is imaginary, as 'imaginary' as the belief in 'magic' ritual. If justice is rooted in the idea that actions have consequences, and if these consequences have been temporarily missed, the only hope is that through ritual re-enactment some measure of redress can be achieved now, in this world, in the present. If actions only have consequences in some immediately unforeseeable future (conceivably when both you and I are long dead), then the opportunity exists for me happily to ignore any potential consequences of my actions in the present. To revisit one's transgressions becomes unhealthy, indicative of psychological fixation. Today, the horror of tragedy could only be conceived in this way. The healthy spirit knows not how to ignore justice per se, but how to believe, magically, that its manifestation comes later. More serious issues are to be attended to, under suitable Machiavellian and pragmatic purchase, in the present. Bradley, *Shakespearean Tragedy*, p. 6.

14. This insight is brought to bear by Cavell in his reading of Thoreau's *Walden*. 'What [we]come to is the learning of resolution. This is what will replace our determination, or commitment, to fate, to the absence of freedom. It is not a matter of doing something new, of determining a course of action and committing ourselves to it, as to jail (II, 5) or to an asylum. Resolution has to do with stillness and with settling (a "clearing," he sometimes calls it). The summary of the writer's learning this is told in his myth of winter, by what happens to him on the ice. It is there that he finds the bottom of the pond, and it is in winter that the owl's prophesy and the fox awaits his transformation.' Winter here is taken as a motif expressing stillness and resolution, away from the dialectics, say, of the greenroom, of springtime. Here Cavell is discussing the narrator of *Walden*, but he might as well be discussing Leontes. Stanley Cavell, *Senses of Walden* (Chicago: University of Chicago Press, 1992), p. 99.

15. No one articulates in more impressive and forceful a manner the antagonism between literary and philosophical 'knowledges' than Tzachi Zamir. He suggests that whatever knowledge contemporary literary studies is after, it is *non-literary*. Astonishingly, he has philosophical criticism picking up the slack of contemporary literary studies, even, in many ways, replacing it *wholesale*. '[P]hilosophical criticism appears to recycle the romantic propensity to perceive the world through emotional and imaginative prisms. Its emphasis on particulars seems to reinvent the "concrete universals" of Ransom and Wimsatt, and it sets the "depth" achieved by reflection through literary works in contrast to the "coldness" of abstract philosophical thought, thus duplicating the opposition between scientific and poetic discourse that figured in the metacritical

writings of Richards, Ransom, and Brooks.' In this case it is the philosopher who is reminding the literary critic that '[f]avourable [philosophical]accounts of rhetoric have also often argued that rationality should not be identified with validity or certainty', and that 'philosophical criticism [now]represents an orientation and sensitivity to the limitations of standard argumentative prose and an attunement to the way these can be overcome through reflection that is interpenetrated with literature'. In a word, philosophy recognises the value of *non-verifiable* knowledge. Elsewhere, Zamir notes, commenting on the debate between Raymond Williams and Lucien Goldmann, that '[a]ccording to Goldmann, most sociology of literature tries to decipher actual consciousness in literary texts, but we should rather look for *possible* consciousness' (my emphasis). Williams is in search of the verifiable, Goldmann of the counterfactual. Tzachi Zamir, *Double Vision: Moral Philosophy and Shakespearean Drama* (Princeton: Princeton University Press, 2007), pp. 45, 23, 47, 49.

Chapter 6

1. Cavell, *Disowning Knowledge*, pp. 125–42.
2. Ibid., p. 134.
3. Sontag, *Against Interpretation*, p. 136.
4. Ibid., p. 6.
5. Jonathan Dollimore, *Radical Tragedy* (New York: Palgrave Macmillan, 2004), p. 189.
6. Ibid., p. 191.
7. Ibid., p. 195.
8. Ibid., p. 202.
9. Ibid., p. 197.

Chapter 7

1. For example, Mark William Roche notes how Hegel's understanding of a character who exists between states of being essentially does not achieve anything we can call 'character'. This, to my mind, suggests that actions are not actions until they are explainable as necessary, which is, ultimately, a denial of character freedom. Mark William Roche, 'Introduction to Hegel's Theory of Tragedy', *PhaenEx* 1.2 (2006), pp. 11–20.
2. Ewan Fernie, 'Introduction', in Fernie, *Spiritual Shakespeares*, p. 15.
3. Ibid., p. 16.
4. The last word goes to Cavell: '[O]ur actions have consequences which outrun our best, and worst intentions. The drama of *King Lear* not merely embodies this theme, it comments on it, even deepens it. For what it shows is that the *reason* consequences furiously hunt us down is not merely that we are half blind, and unfortunate, but that we go on doing the thing which produced these consequences in the first place. What we need is not rebirth, or salvation, but the courage, or plain prudence, to see and to stop. To abdicate. But what do we need in order to do that? It would be salvation' (his emphasis). Cavell, *Disowning Knowledge*, p. 81.

FURTHER READING

Adams, Barry B. *Coming-To-Know: Recognition and the Complex Plot in Shakespeare*. New York: Peter Lang, 2000.

Adelman, Janet. *Suffering Mothers: Fantasies of Maternal Origin in Shakespeare's Plays*. New York: Routledge, 1992.

Armstrong, Paul B. 'The Conflict of Interpretations and the Limits of Pluralism.' *PMLA* 98.3 (1983): 341–52.

Auerbach, Erich. *Mimesis: The Representation of Reality in Western Literature*. Princeton: Princeton University Press, 1968.

Bamber, Linda. *Comic Women, Tragic Men: A Study of Gender and Genre in Shakespeare*. Stanford: Stanford University Press, 1982.

Bayley, John. *Shakespeare and Tragedy*. London: Routledge, 1981.

Bazin, André. *What is Cinema?* Trans. Timothy Barnard. Montreal: Caboose, 2009.

Belsey, Catherine. *The Subject of Tragedy: Identity and Difference in Renaissance Drama*. New York: Methuen, 1985.

——. *Why Shakespeare?* New York: Palgrave Macmillan, 2007.

Bloom, Harold. *The Western Canon*. New York: Riverhead, 1995.

——. 'Foreword.' *Living with Shakespeare*. Ed. Susannah Carson. New York: Knopf Doubleday, 2013. vii–xiv.

Bristol, Michael. *Big-Time Shakespeare*. London: Routledge, 1996.

——. 'How Many Children Did She Have?' *Philosophical Shakespeares*. Ed. John J. Joughin. London: Routledge, 2000. 18–33.

——, ed. *Shakespeare and Moral Agency*. London: Continuum, 2010.

Brooke, Nicholas. *Shakespeare's Early Tragedies*. 1968. London: Methuen, 1973.

Bushnell, Rebecca. *Tragedy: A Short Introduction*. Malden: Blackwell, 2008.

Callaghan, Dympna. *Woman and Gender in Renaissance Tragedy*. Hemel Hempstead: Harvester Wheatsheaf, 1989.

Carroll, Noël. *The Philosophy of Motion Pictures*. Oxford: Blackwell, 2008.

Cavell, Stanley. *Cities of Words*. Cambridge, MA: Harvard Belknap Press, 2004.

——. *Philosophy the Day after Tomorrow*. Cambridge, MA: Harvard Belknap Press, 2005.

——. *The Claim of Reason*. Oxford: Oxford University Press, 1979.

Charney, Maurice, ed. *'Bad' Shakespeare: Revaluations of the Shakespearean Canon*. Toronto: University of Toronto Press, 1988.

Conant, James. 'On Bruns, on Cavell.' *Critical Inquiry* 17.3 (1991): 616–34.

Cooke, Katharine. *A.C. Bradley and His Influence in Twentieth-Century Shakespearean Criticism*. Oxford: Clarendon Press, 1972.

Critchley, Simon. 'Cavell's "Romanticism" and Cavell's Romanticism.' *Contending with Stanley Cavell*. Ed.

Russell B. Goodman. Oxford: Oxford University Press, 2005. 37–54.

Cunningham, J.V. *Woe or Wonder: The Emotional Effect of Shakespearean Tragedy*. Chicago: Swallow Press, 1964.

Danson, Lawrence. *Tragic Alphabet: Shakespeare's Drama of Language*. New Haven: Yale University Press, 1974.

Derrida, Jacques. *Margins of Philosophy*. Chicago: University of Chicago Press, 1982.

——. *Of Grammatology*. Trans. Gayatri Spivak. Baltimore: Johns Hopkins University Press, 1976.

——. *Writing and Difference*. Trans. Alan Bass. London: Routledge, 2001.

Dollimore, Jonathan. 'Response to Neema Parvini.' *Textual Practice* 27.4 (2013): 733–5.

——. 'The Legacy of Cultural Materialism.' *Textual Practice* 27.4 (2013): 715–24.

Donaldson, Jeffrey and Alan Mendelson, eds. *Frye and the Word*. Toronto: University of Toronto Press, 2004.

Drakakis, John, ed. *Alternative Shakespeares*. London: Methuen, 1985.

Dusinberre, Juliet. *Shakespeare and the Nature of Women*. London: Macmillan, 1975.

Eagleton, Terry. *After Theory*. New York: Basic Books, 2003.

——. *William Shakespeare*. New York: Blackwell, 1986.

Eliot, T. S. *The Sacred Wood*. London: Methuen, 1948.

Else, Gerald F. *Aristotle's Poetics: The Argument*. Cambridge, MA: Harvard University Press, 1957.

Evans, Bertrand. *Shakespeare's Tragic Practice*. Oxford: Clarendon Press, 1979.

Evans, Malcolm. *Signifying Nothing: Truth's True Contents in Shakespeare's Text*. Brighton: Harvester, 1989.

Felperin, Howard. *Shakespearean Representation: Mimesis and Modernity in Elizabethan Tragedy*. Princeton: Princeton University Press, 1977.

Ferguson, Niall, ed. *Virtual History: Alternatives and Counterfactuals*. London: Picador, 1997.

Fernie, Ewan. 'Dollimore's Challenge.' *Shakespeare Studies* 35 (2007): 133–57.

Fischer, Michael. *Stanley Cavell and Literary Skepticism*. Chicago: University of Chicago Press, 1989.

French, Marilyn. *Shakespeare's Division of Experience*. New York: Summit, 1981.

Frye, Northrop. *Fools of Time: Studies in Shakespearean Tragedy*. Toronto: University of Toronto Press, 1967.

Garber, Marjorie. 'Shakespeare in Slow Motion.' *Profession* (2010): 151–64.

Girad, René. 'Hamlet's Dull Revenge.' *A Theater of Envy: William Shakespeare*. South Bend: St. Augustine's Press, 2004. 271–89.

——. *The Girard Reader*. Ed. James G. William. New York: Crossroad, 2002.

Grady, Hugh. *Shakespeare, Machiavelli, and Montaigne: Power and Subjectivity from Richard II to Hamlet*. Oxford: Oxford University Press, 2002.

——. *Shakespeare's Universal Wolf: Studies in Early Modern Reification*. Oxford: Clarendon Press, 1996.

Greer, Germaine. *The Female Eunuch*. London: MacGibbon and Kee, 1970.

Happy, Michael. 'The Reality of the Created: From Deconstruction to Recreation.' *Frye and the Word: Religious Contexts in the Writings of Northrop Frye*. Eds Jeffrey Donaldson and Alan Mendelson. Toronto: University of Toronto Press, 2004. 81–96.

Hartley, Andrew James. 'Page and Stage Again: Rethinking Renaissance Character Phenomenologically.' *New Directions in Renaissance Drama and Performance Studies*. Ed. Sarah Werner. New York: Palgrave Macmillan, 2010. 77–93.

Hawkes, Terence, ed. *Alternative Shakespeares*, vol. 2. London: Routledge, 1996.

————. *Shakespeare in the Present.* New York: Routledge, 2002.

Heilman, Robert Bechtold. *Tragedy and Melodrama: Versions of Experience.* Seattle: University of Washington Press, 1968.

Heller, Agnes. 'Historical Truth and Poetic Truth.' *Philosophers on Shakespeare.* Ed. Paul A. Kottman. Stanford: Stanford University Press, 2009. 184–92.

Honigmann, E. A. J. *Shakespeare: Seven Tragedies: The Dramatist's Manipulation of Response.* London: Macmillan, 1976.

Jardine, Lisa. *Still Harping on Daughters: Women and Drama in the Age of Shakespeare.* Brighton: Harvester, 1983.

Jenkins, Harold, ed. *Hamlet.* New York: Arden Shakespeare, 1982.

Johnson, Samuel. 'King Lear'. *Preface to Shakespeare*, by Samuel Johnson. 28 August 2010. University of Adelaide Library. http://ebooks.adelaide.edu.au/j/johnson/samuel/preface/lear.html.

Jones, Emrys. *Scenic Form in Shakespeare.* Oxford: Clarendon Press, 1971.

Jones, Ernest. *Hamlet and Oedipus.* 1949. London: W.W. Norton, 1976.

Kahn, Coppélia. *Man's Estate: Masculine Identity in Shakespeare.* Berkeley: University of California Press, 1981.

Kaufmann, Walter. *Tragedy and Philosophy.* Princeton: Princeton University Press, 1968.

Lynch, Jack, ed. *King Lear: Adapted by Nahum Tate.* N.d. Rutgers University, Newark. http://ethnicity.rutgers.edu/~jlynch/Texts/tatelear.html.

Muir, Kenneth. *Shakespeare's Tragic Sequence.* Liverpool: Liverpool University Press, 1979.

Nevo, Ruth. *Tragic Form in Shakespeare*. Princeton: Princeton University Press, 1972.

Nuttall, A. D. *Why Does Tragedy Give Pleasure?* Oxford: Oxford University Press, 1996.

Oort, Richard van. 'Hamlet's Theatre of Envy.' *The Originary Hypothesis*. Ed. Adam Katz. Aurora: Davies Group, 2007. 151–69.

Pocock, J. G. A. *The Machiavellian Moment: Florentine Political Thought and the Atlantic Republican Tradition*. Princeton: Princeton University Press, 1975.

Popper, Karl. *The Poverty of Historicism*. 1957. London: Routledge, 2002.

Price, Hereward. *Construction in Shakespeare*. Ann Arbor: University of Michigan Press, 1951.

Rabkin, Norman. *Shakespeare and the Common Understanding*. 1967. Chicago: University of Chicago Press, 1984.

Ricoeur, Paul. *Freud and Philosophy: An Essay on Interpretation*. Trans. Denis Savage. New Haven: Yale University Press, 1970.

Rorty, Richard. 'Cavell on Skepticism.' *Contending with Stanley Cavell*. Ed. Russell B. Goodman. Oxford: Oxford University Press, 2005. 10–21.

Sanders, Wilbur. *The Dramatist and the Received Idea*. Cambridge: Cambridge University Press, 1968.

Shakespeare, William. *Othello*. Ed. Kim F. Hall. Boston: Bedford/St. Martin's, 2007.

——. *The Winter's Tale*. Ed. Mario DiGangi. Boston: Bedford/St. Martin's, 2008.

Simkin, Stevie. *Early Modern Tragedy and the Cinema of Violence*. Houndmills: Palgrave Macmillan, 2006.

Snyder, Susan. *The Comic Matrix of Shakespeare's Tragedies*. Princeton: Princeton University Press, 1979.

Steinkraus, Warren E., ed. *New Studies in Hegel*. Holt: Rinehart & Winston, 1971.

Stoll, E.E. *Art and Artifice in Shakespeare*. New York: Barnes & Noble, 1962.

Vickers, Brian. *Appropriating Shakespeare: Contemporary Critical Quarrels*. New Haven: Yale University Press, 1993.

Williams, Raymond. *Modern Tragedy*. London: Chatto & Windus, 1966.

Yachnin, Paul. *Stage-Wrights: Shakespeare, Jonson, Middleton, and the Making of Theatrical Value*. Philadelphia: University of Philadelphia Press, 1997.

INDEX